SIXTH EDITION

The
iPhone
How to do the most important,
useful & fun stuff with your iPhone Book

Scott Kelby & Terry White

The iPhone Book, Sixth Edition

The iPhone Book Team

CREATIVE DIRECTOR
Felix Nelson

PRODUCTION MANAGER
Dave Damstra

TECHNICAL EDITORS
Kim Doty
Cindy Snyder

ART DIRECTOR
Jessica Maldonado

ALL PHOTOGRAPHY
Scott Kelby
Terry White

PUBLISHED BY
Peachpit Press

Copyright © 2013 by Scott Kelby

Composed in Myriad Pro and Helvetica Neue by Kelby Media Group.

Trademarks
All terms mentioned in this book that are known to be trademarks or service marks have been appropriately capitalized. Peachpit Press cannot attest to the accuracy of this information. Use of a term in the book should not be regarded as affecting the validity of any trademark or service mark.

iPhone, iPod, iTunes, iPad, Macintosh, and Mac are registered trademarks of Apple. Windows is a registered trademark of Microsoft Corporation.

Warning and Disclaimer
This book is designed to provide information about the iPhone. Every effort has been made to make this book as complete and as accurate as possible, but no warranty of fitness is implied.

The information is provided on an as-is basis. The authors and Peachpit Press shall have neither liability nor responsibility to any person or entity with respect to any loss or damages arising from the information contained in this book or from the use of the discs, electronic files, or programs that may accompany it.

ISBN: 13: 978-0-321-90856-8
ISBN: 10:   0-321-90856-2

9 8 7 6 5 4 3 2

Printed and bound in the United States of America

http://kelbytraining.com
www.peachpit.com

For my dear friend Dave Gales,
an iPhone fanatic from the start
and one of the best guys on the planet.
–SCOTT KELBY

For my mom, who always taught me to do the right thing,
and for my dad, who inspired me and pushed me to succeed.
I also dedicate this book to Steve Jobs. If it were not for his
vision and determination, the iPhone and many other
tech gifts that enhance our lives would not exist.
–TERRY WHITE

Scott's Acknowledgments

This is the seventh book I've been lucky enough to co-author with Terry, and I can tell you from experience that the only downside of co-authoring a book with him is that I only get half as much space to thank all the wonderful people whose help, hard work, and support go into making a book like this.

To Kalebra: My wonderful, amazing, hilarious, fun-filled, super-gorgeous, and loving wife. Your spirit, warmth, beauty, brains, patience, and unconditional love continue to prove what everybody always says—I'm the luckiest guy in the world.

To Jordan & Kira: You two bring immeasurable joy to my life, and I'm so proud and tickled to be your dad. I couldn't ask for anything more.

To Jeff: You are the world standard that all brothers should be judged by. No wonder everybody loves you the way they do!

To my co-author Terry White: You're the one who convinced me to do this book, and without your many ideas, your influence, and your great writing, this book would never have seen the light of day. I'm truly honored to have shared these pages with you, and to count you among my very best friends.

To Susan Hageanon: Thanks for finding a way to carve out time for me to be able to write this book in the first place. I know it's not easy assisting someone who is constantly in stealth mode, but you're doing a great job of it and I appreciate it more than you know.

To my editor Kim Doty: I just love working with you. How can you not love working with someone who always has such a warm smile, such a great attitude, and does such great work? Thanks doesn't cover it…but…thanks.

To Cindy Snyder and Jessica Maldonado (my book editing, design, and layout team): I just love working with you guys, and I'm constantly impressed and amazed at the quality of what you do and how quickly you can do it.

To Felix Nelson, my brilliant Creative Director: What can I say? You are the best in the business and ideas and art flow out of you like a Pez dispenser. I'm a very lucky guy to even get to work with you. Thank you, my friend, for everything you do for me and our company.

To Dave Moser: Getting to work with my best buddy every day is definitely a blessing, but the way you're always looking out for me takes it to a whole new level. :-)

To Jean A. Kendra: Thanks for watching "the other side" of our business and for being such a great friend over the years.

To Nancy Aldrich-Ruenzel, Ted Waitt, Sara Jane Todd, Scott Cowlin, and all my friends at Peachpit Press: Thank you for making the book-writing process virtually painless, and for having me as one of your authors.

To John Graden, Jack Lee, Dave Gales, Judy Farmer, and Douglas Poole: Your wisdom and whip-cracking have helped me immeasurably throughout my life, and I'm both grateful and totally in your debt.

To God and His Son Jesus Christ: Thank You for always hearing my prayers, for always being there when I need You, for blessing me with such a wonderful, joy-filled life, and such a warm, loving family to share it with.

Terry's Acknowledgments

It's not every day that I get to work on a project that is both challenging and fun at the same time. Writing a book such as this takes a lot of focus and attention to detail, but my family didn't complain once.

I have two amazing daughters: Ayoola is both smart and constantly focused on taking it to the next level. I see so much of myself in her at times that it's scary. My youngest daughter, Sala, has many of my other traits. She makes me laugh out loud every day and lives to enjoy life. They make those late nights, weekends spent working, and hectic travel schedules worthwhile, because at the end of the day, it's all for them anyway.

I have a great sister, Pam, who is the person I go to when I need advice. It's great having an older sibling and she's the best sister a guy could have.

I have to thank all my "gadget buddies"! It's the guys and gals that I hang out with that inspire me to play and learn about gadgets of all kinds. Special thanks to Sarah K for always keeping me up to date with the latest tunes and apps that I may have missed. Speaking of apps, I have to thank both my co-authors on www.bestappsite.com, Erik Bernskiold and Jason Lykins, because I couldn't do it without their help.

If technology is my first passion, then I would have to say that photography is my second. While the iPhone is my go-to device for daily communications and social networking, I also use it and my iPad quite extensively in my photography workflows. With that said, I can't help but thank those individuals that I work with and photograph on a regular basis, starting with the amazing Zahava for the hard work in modeling for this book and other projects. Thanks to Kandice Lynn, who's a blast to work with and inspires me to push my photography further. I also want to thank my amazing designer, W. Taharqa Blue, and video buddies, Bruce Mandel and Don Pham, as well as all the photography industry leaders that have shown me so much support over the years.

Also, I thank my friends at my local Apple Store, Linda and Dave, for constantly making me feel like a VIP when I walk in. And, of course, I have to thank all my friends who support me at my Macintosh users' group, MacGroup-Detroit, especially Joe, Calvin, Jack, Chita, Phyllis, Yvonne, Bill, Brian & Char, Mia, Michele, Steve, Mike, Aquil, and Harold.

Although I enjoy writing, it's not my full-time gig. I have the best job on the planet and work for the best company in the world. I have to give special thanks to my boss, Scott Morris, who understands my gadget addictions and gives me the freedom and the time off that I need to pursue my other technology and industry passions. I work with some of the smartest people in the industry, and I want to thank everyone at Adobe Systems, Inc., including my travel buddies, Worldwide Evangelists Jason Levine and Rufus Deuchler, not only for providing the best software tools in existence but also for keeping me technically educated and motivated to achieve greatness.

Of course, I have to thank the guy who is probably my biggest source of inspiration, and that is one of my best friends and the co-author of this book, Scott Kelby. I'm constantly amazed at how much this guy accomplishes each year. There is no stopping him. Not only is he great in his career, but he's also a great father to his two beautiful kids and a great husband to his wonderful wife, Kalebra. I probably wouldn't have gotten into all this writing if it wasn't for Scott. Scott, you're an inspiration to us all! Thanks, buddy!

About the Authors

Scott Kelby

Scott is Editor-in-Chief and Publisher of *Photoshop User* magazine, and co-host of *The Grid*, the weekly talk show for photographers. He is President and co-founder of the National Association of Photoshop Professionals (NAPP), the trade association for Adobe® Photoshop® users, and President of the software, education, and publishing firm Kelby Media Group.

Scott is a photographer, designer, and award-winning author of more than 50 books on technology and digital imaging, including the best-selling books: *The iPod Book*, *The Digital Photography Book*, parts 1, 2, 3, and 4, and *The Adobe Photoshop Book for Digital Photographers*. Scott has authored several best-selling Macintosh books, including the award-winning *Macintosh: The Naked Truth*, from New Riders, and *The Mac OS X Leopard Book* and *Mac OS X Killer Tips* from Peachpit Press. His books have been translated into dozens of different languages, including Russian, Chinese, French, German, Spanish, Korean, Greek, Turkish, Japanese, Dutch, and Taiwanese, among others.

For six years straight, Scott was awarded the distinction of being the world's #1 best-selling author of all computer and technology books, across all categories, and for the past two years, he was named the #1 best-selling author of books on photography. His book, *The Digital Photography Book*, volume 1, is the best-selling book on digital photography of all time.

Scott is Training Director for the Adobe Photoshop Seminar Tour, Conference Technical Chair for the Photoshop World Conference & Expo, and is a speaker at trade shows and events around the world. For more information on Scott, visit him at:

His daily blog: http://scottkelby.com
Google+: Scottgplus.com
Twitter: http://twitter.com@scottkelby
Facebook: www.facebook.com/skelby

Terry White

Terry is the author of *Secrets of Adobe Bridge* from Adobe Press and co-author of *InDesign CS/CS2 Killer Tips*, from New Riders.

Terry is Worldwide Creative Suite Design Evangelist for Adobe Systems, Inc., and has been with Adobe for over a decade, where he leads the charge in evangelizing and showing Adobe's Creative Suite products to users around the world. Terry is both an Adobe Certified Expert and Creative Suite Master.

He has been active in the industry for over 25 years and is the founder and President of MacGroup-Detroit, Michigan's largest Macintosh users' group, and is a columnist for *Photoshop User* magazine.

Terry is the host of the top-ranked *Adobe Creative Suite Video Podcast* (http://creativesuitepodcast.com) and author of the world renown *Best App Site* (your source for iPhone, iPad, and iPod touch app news and reviews; www.bestappsite.com), *Terry White's Tech Blog* (http://terrywhite.com), and is a key presenter at major industry shows around the world.

Follow him on Twitter—@TerryLWhite—and **Like his Facebook page** at http://facebook.com/TerryWhiteFans.

Chapter Three   **53**

Message in a Bottle
Sending Text Messages

Chapter Four   **71**

App Anthem
Using Apps & the App Store

Chapter Five   **85**

Please Mr. Postman
Getting (and Sending) Email

(Continued)

http://kelbytraining.com

http://kelbytraining.com

Chapter Eight   **169**

Let's Get Siri-us
How to Use Siri: Your Built-In Personal Assistant

Chapter Nine   **179**

McCloud
Keep Everything in Sync Using iCloud

(Continued)

http://kelbytraining.com

Chapter Thirteen **257**

Cereal Killer
Killer Tips and Tricks

(Continued)

http://kelbytraining.com

http://kelbytraining.com

Chapter Fifteen   323

The Trouble with Boys
Troubleshooting Your iPhone

Chapter Sixteen   343

Matchbox Twenty
20 Apps We Can't Live Without

http://kelbytraining.com

Seven Things You'll Wish You Had Known...

(1) The first chapter is for people brand new to the iPhone (you just opened the box), so if you've had your iPhone for a few weeks and you already know how to turn it on, how to zoom in, how to get around, put it to sleep, etc., you can skip right over to Chapter 2 and start there. It won't hurt our feelings one bit (but you might want to at least skim through Chapter 1 anyway. Hey, ya never know).

(2) You don't have to read it chapter by chapter. Outside of that first I-just-opened-the-box chapter, we designed this to be a "jump-in-anywhere" book. You don't have to read it in order, chapter by chapter—if you want to learn how to do a certain thing, just find it in the Table of Contents, turn to that page, and you'll have the answer in seconds. Each page shows you how to do just one important thing. One topic. One idea. For example, if you want to learn how to delete an email, we will show you, step by step, how to do exactly that. No big discussions about email account protocols, or about server-side instructions—just how to delete an email message. That's it.

(3) We didn't totally "geek out." Terry and I wrote everything just as if a friend came over to our house, pulled out their new iPhone, and started asking questions. So, for example, if you were at my house and you turned to me and said, "Hey Scott, is there a way to see more of this webpage on my screen?" I wouldn't go into how the iPhone's built-in vibrotactile actuator works. In real life, I'd turn to you and say, "Just turn your iPhone sideways and it switches to give you a wider view." I'd tell you short, sweet, and right to the point, just like that. So that's what we do throughout the book. It's not a "tell-me-all-about-it" book, instead it's a "show-me-how-to-do-it" book.

Before Reading This Book!

(4) There's a bonus chapter just for you. We know one of the most fun parts of the iPhone experience is the downloadable apps (both from Apple themselves and from third-party developers), so Terry and I got together and added a bonus chapter with our own picks for the "20 Apps We Can't Live Without." Of course, it's possible you'll be able to live without all or any of these, but then you'd be leading a shallow, empty shell of a life and now that we're friends (hey, you bought our book), we just couldn't let that happen. Most of them are either free or pretty cheap (just like me and Terry ;-).

(5) The intro page at the beginning of each chapter is designed to give you a quick mental break, and honestly, they have little to do with the chapter. In fact, they have little to do with anything, but writing these off-the-wall chapter intros is kind of a tradition of mine (I do this in all my books), but if you're one of those really "serious" types, you can skip them because they'll just get on your nerves.

(6) One bonus chapter is just not enough! Although we put lots of cool tips (we call 'em "iTips") throughout the book, you can never have enough tips (stuff like little-known shortcuts, suggestions, or tricks that can make using your iPhone easier or more fun), so in this sixth edition of the book, there's a special bonus chapter of nothing but "killer" tips (Chapter 13).

(7) If your iPhone's screen doesn't look like what you see here, then you haven't updated it with the free iOS 6 software from Apple. So, just connect your iPhone to your computer, launch Apple's iTunes, and you'll get a dialog telling you about the new software (or go to Software Update in your iPhone's General settings to update wirelessly). Just click Download and Install, and everything will look like what you see here in the book. Okay, that's it—you're ready to roll!

slide to unlock

Chapter One

The Bare Essentials

10 Things Brand New iPhone Users Need to Know

If you've already been using your iPhone for a few weeks, skip right to Chapter 2

 It's a tradition of mine to name my chapters after movie, TV show, or song titles, so I was originally going to name this chapter *Basic Training* after the 1985 movie by the same name (or the 1971 version of *Basic Training*, or the 2006 version, which went straight to video despite the fact it starred The Rock). But I started to wonder how many people would actually read a chapter that has the word "basic" in the title. It's sad, but nobody really wants to learn the basics anymore—they want to jump into the deep end of the pool and start with some advanced techniques, because they figure the basic stuff is too basic for them. So basically, I thought instead about using the title from the movie *Basic Instinct*. Now, I never actually saw the movie myself (didn't it have Scatman Crothers in it?), but I heard it was better than *Basic Instinct 2*, which I think starred Carrot Top and Ernest Borgnine (but since I didn't see that one either, I can't swear they were actually in it). So I started thinking of a term that meant basics but didn't have the downside of the word basics, and I came up with "essentials." Because this chapter covers the essential stuff you'll need to really make the most of your iPhone, but "essentials" has no marketing flair. No pizzaz. No bling. (No bling?) So I thought, what device do American marketers use to capture the attention of today's most coveted demographic (people with credit left on their Visa cards), and then *Bare Essentials* (from the short-lived 1991 TV series of the same name) came to mind. It sounds just naughty enough to trick someone into reading it, but not so naughty that Snoop Dogg would read it. That brings up an interesting question. What are you doing here?

Turning Your iPhone On, Off, and Putting It to Sleep

To turn on your iPhone, press-and-hold the **Sleep/Wake button** at the top (shown circled here in red on the left). After a moment, the Apple logo will appear, and then you'll get the Unlock screen. Press lightly on the arrow button, and slide it to the right to get to the Home screen, which is your main jumping off point to all the different things the iPhone can do. To turn your iPhone completely off, press-and-hold the Sleep/Wake button for around four seconds and a red **Slide to Power Off button** will appear (shown above right). Press lightly on it and slide it to the right. Your screen will turn black, you'll see a small round status icon for just a moment, then your iPhone will power off. To save battery life when you're not using the iPhone, press the **Sleep/Wake button** once to put it to sleep—you'll hear a little click sound, then your screen will go black (don't worry—it will still receive calls and text messages). To wake it from sleep, either press that button again, or press the Home button (the round "real" button just below the screen). By the way, if you're not doing anything on your iPhone, in about 45 seconds, it dims the brightness of the screen (to save battery), and then about 15 seconds later, if you still haven't done anything, it puts itself to sleep.

---

iTip **Canceling the Shutdown**

*If you get to the "power down" screen and then decide you didn't want to actually turn off your iPhone after all, just tap the **Cancel button** and it will go back to the screen you were on. If you do nothing for about 30 seconds, that will also cancel the shutdown.*

Using Your iPhone's Touchscreen

The touchscreen on your iPhone works amazingly well, and there are just a few little things to learn to make the most of it. Here are the three biggies:

(1) You don't have to press hard. It just takes a light tap on the touchscreen to launch an app (short for application), to choose any button, or select anything. It's surprisingly sensitive, which is great.

(2) You can zoom in much closer on part of a webpage, or email message, or photo, etc., by either: (a) double-tapping on the area you want to zoom in on, or (b) "pinching out," which is where you pinch your index finger and thumb together, then touch the screen with them pinched together, and then spread them apart. As you spread out your fingers, the screen zooms in. To zoom back out, start with your fingers apart—touch the top of the screen with your index finger and the bottom with your thumb—and pinch inward until they touch (like you're trying to pinch the screen).

(3) To scroll, or move something (like a slider), you touch the screen lightly and just "swipe" from left to right across the screen (Apple calls this "flicking," but it feels more like a swipe to me). For example, to see the album art in your iPhone's Music app, just touch an album lightly with your finger and kind of flick it (like you're flipping pages in a book). To scroll or move faster, swipe faster.

Getting Back to the Home Screen

The Home screen is pretty much your starting off point for…well…everything. It's where all your apps are, and it's where you go first to do everything from making a call to playing a song, so you need a quick way to get there. So, how important is getting to the Home screen? Well, there's only one "hard" button (an actual real button you can feel) on the face of the iPhone (it's found just below the touchscreen), and its main job is to take you to the Home screen, no matter what else you're doing. Just press it once, and the Home screen appears (as seen above). Of course, if you press it more than once, other stuff happens, but we'll cover that later. For now, know that you're always just one click away from this Home screen.

Making Phone Calls

Start at the Home screen, then tap on Phone. To dial a number, tap the **Keypad button**, and a standard telephone keypad appears. Now, just dial the number you want (it even makes those tone dialing sounds when you dial the number), and tap the green Call button. To end a call, tap the red End button. If you make a mistake while dialing the number, tap the Back button (to the right of the Call button). Before you make the call, if you want to add the number of the person you're about to call to your contacts list (your address book, basi-cally), then tap the button to the left of the Call button, and it brings up a menu where you can create a new contact for the person at this number, or add it to a contact you've already created (much more on this, and all the cool features of the iPhone's phone, are in Chapter 2). One more thing: If somebody calls you, trust me—without any further explanation, you'll know what to do (see above right).

---

iTip Switching to Silent Mode

*If you want to switch your iPhone to Silent mode, just move the **Ring/Silent switch** (found on the top-left side of your iPhone) toward the back of the iPhone—you'll see a large icon appear onscreen. Switch back to regular Ring mode by moving the Ring/Silent switch back toward the screen side of your iPhone.*

Using Your iPhone's Built-In Speaker

Just tap the **Speaker button** that appears onscreen while your call is in progress. When you tap that button, it will turn solid blue to let you know the speakerphone is active. To turn the speakerphone off, tap that solid blue button again.

iTip   **Keeping Your iPhone Private**

Want to keep the info on your iPhone private? Then password protect it, so each time it wakes from sleep it asks you to input your secret four-digit password. To learn how to do this, see Chapter 7.

How to Send Text Messages

Start at the Home screen, then tap Messages. The first time you send a text message, this will take you directly to the New Message screen, where you can type and send your text. After that, tapping Messages will take you to your Messages list. So, to send a text message from there, tap the button in the top-right corner of the screen (it looks like a page with a pencil on it). In the To field, enter the phone number (or just a name if they're already in your contacts list—more on your contacts list in Chapter 2), then tap once in the field to the right of the camera icon and type in your text. (Hey, what's the camera icon for? See Chapter 3 for more on that kind of stuff.) When you're done with your message, just tap the green **Send button** (it will be blue if you're texting another iPhone user) and your message is on its way (a little Sending status bar appears on the top of the screen, so you can see the progress of your message being sent). That's the bare bones basics on texting, but if you turn to Chapter 3, you'll find lots more cool stuff your iPhone can do.

> **iTip   If You Miss a Call or a Text Message**
>
> *If your iPhone is asleep and you miss a text message or call, it keeps track of all this stuff in the Notification Center, which makes it easy for you to quickly see what you missed. To get to these alerts, just go to the top of your screen and swipe downward to see the Notification Center. In it, you'll see a list of what you missed, any calendar event, weather, and stocks. If you want to reply to a text, voicemail, etc., listed there, just tap on it and it takes you right to that app.*

Using the Built-In Keyboard

Anytime you need to type something on your iPhone, a keyboard automatically appears onscreen. The keys are kind of small, but as you type, a large version of the letter you just typed pops up in front of your finger so you can see instantly if you hit the right letter. I can tell you from experience that the more you use this keyboard, the easier it gets, so if you wind up misspelling just about every word when you first start, don't sweat it—in just a couple of days, you'll be misspelling only every third or fourth word. There's also a pretty clever Auto-Correction function. Although it will suggest a word while you're typing it, go ahead and finish the word (especially if you've spelled it wrong) and it will replace your misspelled word with the correct word (95% of the time). You do have to get used to typing a word, seeing that you've misspelled it, and continuing to type. If you do that, you'll be amazed at how quickly you'll be able to type using this keyboard.

iTip **Fixing Your Typos**

If you need to go back and fix a typo that the Auto-Correction feature didn't catch, just press-and-hold approximately where the typo occurred and a magnifying Loupe appears onscreen so you can not only clearly see the location of your cursor, but you can move the cursor with your finger, as well, to quickly let you fix the mistake.

Downloading Songs/Videos Right to Your iPhone

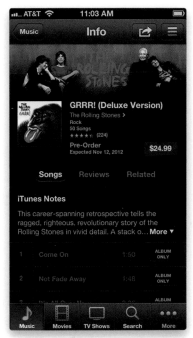

You can wirelessly download songs, TV shows, movies, podcasts, music videos, and more, using the iTunes app. It comes pre-installed on your iPhone, and you'll find it on the Home screen—just tap once on iTunes and it takes you to the iTunes Store. Once you're there, it's easy to find songs and videos to buy or rent, and then download directly to your iPhone (for more on using the iTunes Store, see Chapter 10, but for now, I just wanted to let you know that you can buy music and videos, right from your iPhone, without having to use your computer at all).

Flipping Your View

Because the iPhone is a phone, you probably wind up holding it vertically (tall), like you would any other phone, but the iPhone was the first phone to let you turn it on its side, automatically changing your view to widescreen. This is incredibly handy when watching movies (well, it's more than handy—it automatically plays movies in the wide view, so you'll want to turn your iPhone on its side for sure), but beyond that, it makes the touch-screen keyboard larger, you can see more of webpages, your photos are larger, you can see more of your emails (you get the picture). Most apps support a wide view, so just give it a shot—turn your iPhone sideways and it immediately changes your view to widescreen. Sweet!

Charging Your iPhone

There are two ways to charge your iPhone: (1) the AC power adapter (one end plugs into the dock connector at the bottom of your iPhone using the white USB cable that came with it, and the other end plugs into a standard household outlet), or (2) your iPhone will also charge anytime it's connected to your computer (you use that same USB cable, but you pull off the power plug on the end to reveal a standard USB plug. So, one end plugs into the dock connector on the bottom of your iPhone, and the other end plugs into the USB port on your computer). When your iPhone is charging, the little battery icon at the top right of the screen will display a lightning bolt icon on it. When the battery is fully charged, it will change into a power plug icon, instead. (Note: There are other ways to charge it, like car chargers, but you have to buy those separately. Also, although, in the past, Apple has made a Universal Dock, that you can just sit your iPhone in and it stands upright while charging, at the time this book was published, Apple had not yet announced a version for the iPhone 5.)

iTip	Charging Via Your Computer

While you can charge your iPhone directly from the USB port on your computer, the battery may drain, not charge, when the computer goes to sleep or is in hibernation mode. You also may not get enough power if you connect your iPhone to a USB hub—it's usually best to connect it directly to your computer's built-in USB port.

Chapter Two

Phoneheads

How to Use the Phone

 I thought "Phoneheads" was a great name for this chapter, but it's not the name of a song; it's the name of a band that plays electronic music, which is why you probably haven't heard of them. My guess is that you don't listen to much electronic music. I'm not talking about music made with electronics (like electric guitars or synths), I'm talking about the kind of music you hear your teenagers playing, and you shake your head in disgust telling them, "That's not music!" Then one day, when you hear Van Halen's "Jamie's Cryin'" playing on your oldies station, you look in your rear view mirror and tell your kids, "Now that's music!" The sad thing is—you're right. That was music. And the stuff kids are listening to today is nothing more than an aural assault on everything we hold sacred about "real" music, which includes: white headbands, skinny ties, parachute pants, big hair, the hood of Whitesnake's car, inexpensive gas, and cassette tapes. Now *that* was music. I'm pretty safe in saying all this because you bought an iPhone, which means you must be pretty well off (or just incredibly loose with money), because iPhones aren't cheap. That means you're probably in your late 30s or early 40s, and you think that electronic music isn't music, so when I wrote that earlier, you were nodding your head. But, there is a second scenario: one in which you're young, and have rich parents, and they bought you an iPhone because they're loose with money. In that case, make sure you check out Phonehead's track "Syrinx (TGM Mix)." I love that song!

Importing Contacts

If you've got your contacts already on your Mac or PC, getting those contacts onto your iPhone is a breeze using Apple's iTunes (it comes pre-installed on every Mac, and it's a free download from Apple's website for Windows users). iTunes lets you automatically sync your contacts from your Address Book application or Yahoo! Address Book on a Mac and from Windows Contacts on a PC. You can also sync from Microsoft Outlook or Google Contacts on both platforms. If you're a corporate user on a Microsoft Exchange server, you can get your contacts over the air, as well (see your IT department for the settings). Just connect your iPhone to your computer using the USB cable that came with it and then launch iTunes on your computer. Click on your iPhone under Devices on the left side of the iTunes window, click the Info button at the top, then turn on the Sync Contacts checkbox at the top of the Info screen, and click the Sync button in the bottom-right corner.

Note: If you are getting contacts through your iCloud account, you can set your iPhone to sync through the iCloud settings in the Settings app. (See Chapter 9 for more on this.) Also, if you are using a webmail email account that includes contacts (like Hotmail or Yahoo!) on your iPhone, you can sync them by tapping on the Settings app, tapping on Mail, Contacts, Calendars, tapping on the webmail account, and turning Contacts on.

Importing Contacts from Your Old Cell Phone

The first step is to transfer the contacts from your old phone onto your computer. Then you can go back to the previous page and follow those instructions to get those contacts from your computer to your iPhone. If your old phone doesn't automatically sync with your computer, then go to www.markspace.com and use the their Missing Sync utility for the particular phone you have (they support everything from a BlackBerry to a Nokia, and about everything in-between). You just tell them (using the pop-up menus) which brand your old cell phone is and which model, and they will take you to the right sync utility to get your contacts off your old phone and onto your computer.

Importing Your Google Contacts on Your iPhone

If you use Google's popular Gmail, you can sync the contacts you have there with your iPhone from right on the iPhone itself. Tap on the Settings app, then tap on **Mail, Contacts, Calendars**. Tap Add Account, then tap Microsoft Exchange (I know that part sounds weird, but stick with me here). In the Email field, type in your full Gmail address, then enter your password, and then in the Description field, go ahead and name this "Gmail" just so you know what it is. Tap the Next button in the top-right corner and it verifies that your info is correct. On the Exchange screen, you'll see a Server field where you need to enter "m.google .com." Ignore the Domain field, and then enter your Gmail username (don't include the @gmail.com part—just the username itself). Your password has already been entered, so tap the Next button again. On the next screen, it will ask if you want to sync your mail, contacts, or calendars. In this case, turn off Mail and Calendars (unless, of course, you want those, too), turn on Contacts, then tap the Save button at the top right, and voilà—your Gmail contacts are now on your iPhone.

Importing Your Contacts from Facebook

Luckily, getting your Facebook contacts into your iPhone's Contacts app may be easier than getting them from anywhere else, because when you install the Facebook app (just tap on the Settings app, then scroll down, tap on Facebook, then tap Install), then enter your username and password, it's ready to import your Facebook contacts onto your iPhone. Just tap the **Update All Contacts** button and it does the rest. Easy peasy.

---

iTip **Dealing with Duplicates in Your Contacts App**

*If you're downloading contacts from multiple places (like, for example, from Gmail and Facebook), you're likely to have a few duplicates. Easy enough to fix: When you find a duplicate in the Contacts app, tap the Edit button at the top right, then tap the **Link Contact button** at the bottom. Choose the duplicate contact, then tap the Link button at the top right, then tap the Done button. This merges the two contacts into just one.*

Adding New Contacts from Scratch

If you want to create a new contact from scratch, tap on the Phone app, then tap on the Contacts button, and tap the **+ (plus sign) button** in the upper-right-hand corner to bring up a New Contact screen. Tap on the info you want to add. For example, to add your new contact's email address, just tap on Home Email and you can then type in their email address using the keyboard at the bottom of the screen (you can also change Home to Work or Other by tapping on it and choosing a new label in the list that pops up). When you're done adding the email address, scroll up and down and add more info the same way. When you're finished adding the new contact info, tap the Done button in the top-right corner.

---

iTip **Getting Back to the Previous Screen**

Here's a tip to help you think like your iPhone: most of the time, if you see a button in the upper-left corner of the screen, it acts like a Back button in a web browser—pressing it will take you back to the previous screen you were on.

Search for a Contact

When you go to your contacts list (from the Phone app or the Contacts app), there will be a **Search field** at the top of the list. Tap in it to get the keyboard, start typing the name of the contact you're looking for, and the iPhone will immediately begin narrowing down the list to names that match what you've typed. Once you see the name you're looking for, you can stop typing and tap the contact you found to bring up their Info screen. You can also do a system-wide search using the **Spotlight feature** by either pressing the Home button from the first Home screen or by swiping to the right from your first Home screen.

---

iTip **Narrowing Down Your Search**

If you want to narrow the list down even further, type the first letter of the first name, then type a space, and then type the first letter of the last name. This will narrow the list down to only the contacts with those initials. You can still keep typing to get to the name you want. So if you wanted to find Scott Kelby, you'd type "S Kel" and that would narrow the list down quicker than having to scroll through multiple Scotts.

Dialing Someone in Your Contacts List

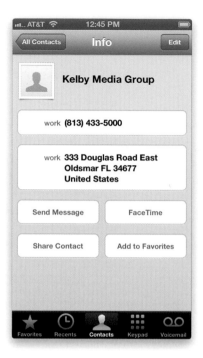

Tap on the Phone app, then tap on the **Contacts button** (okay, that was pretty obvious), and then tap on the person's name in the list. This brings up their full contact info, including a list of all their phone numbers you have added (cell number, home, office, etc.). To dial one of those numbers, just tap once on it and it starts dialing.

iTip **Jumping Right to a Letter**

When you're in the All Contacts list, if you want to jump directly to a particular letter quickly, just tap once on the letter in the alphabetic list on the far-right side of the screen. You can also tap, hold, and slide up/down the list, as well.

Seeing a Contact's Photo When They Call

Tap on the Phone app, then the Contacts button. Scroll to the contact you want to assign a photo to, tap their name, then tap the Edit button in the top-right corner of the screen. In the upper-left corner of the Info screen, tap on Add Photo. This brings up two buttons: **Take Photo** (so you can take a photo of your contact using your iPhone's camera), and **Choose Photo** (which lets you choose any photo you've already taken with or imported into your iPhone). If you tap the Choose Photo button, it takes you to your Photos screen, where you can find the photo you want and tap on it to assign to your contact. You'll get a screen where you can choose the size and position of the photo that will display when your contact calls (use your finger to slide it around, which basically crops the photo, or "pinch it" with your fingers to scale it up or down). When it looks good to you, tap the gray Choose button and you're done. If, instead, you tap the Take Photo button, just take the photo, scale and move it, and tap Use Photo. This is cool, but the picture won't be in the Camera Roll for download later. So if it's a picture you will want to use for something else, take the picture first and add it to the contact afterward.

Dialing a Call

If you want to dial a number, tap on the Phone app, then tap on the **Keypad button** to bring up the dialing buttons you see above. To dial a number, just tap the number keys. If you make a mistake, press the Back button (the button to the right of the green Call button) to erase that digit. Once you've dialed the correct number, tap the **Call button**.

---

iTip   **Redialing a Number**

*If you want to redial the last number you manually dialed, in the Phone app, tap the Keypad button and then tap **Call**. This will display the last number you dialed manually and tapping Call again will actually dial it.*

The Advantage of Using Groups

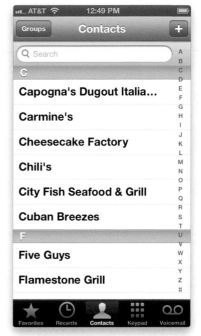

Most contact managers on your computer (including Apple's Address Book application) allow you to have contact groups (like one group for your friends, and maybe one for co-workers, and one for restaurants, so you don't have to dig through all your contacts every time). Well, if you've set up groups like that on your computer, you can have those same groups on your iPhone to making finding contacts even easier (and they sync to your phone automatically if you have it set up this way). Now, to access these groups, tap on the Phone app, then tap on Contacts, then tap the **Groups button** (in the upper-left corner) to see a list of your different groups. Then, you can tap on the groups that you don't want to see (to turn them off) and tap the Done button to see just those contacts in the group you do want to see (like seeing just your favorite restaurants, as shown above).

Setting Up Your Speed Dial Favorites

Your iPhone's name for speed dial is "Favorites," and to turn one of your contacts into a Favorite, just tap on their name in your contacts list to view the screen with their full contact info. Then, in the bottom-right corner of their Info screen, tap on the **Add to Favorites button** (shown circled here in red), and then choose whether to add that contact as a Voice Call or FaceTime favorite. Now, there is another way to do it, and that is to start at the Favorites screen (in the Phone app, tap the Favorites button), then tap the little **+ (plus sign) button** in the upper-right corner. This brings up your contacts list, and you just tap on the name of the contact you want added to your Favorites. If your contact has only one phone number (like just a home number, or just a cell number), then you'll just have to choose whether to add them as a Voice Call or FaceTime favorite, and they're immediately added as a Favorite. If they have multiple numbers, then it brings up all their numbers and you just tap on the number you want added as a Favorite.

Reordering (or Removing) Favorites

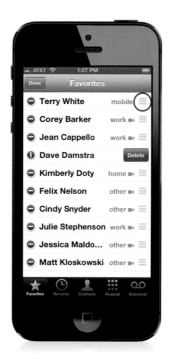

Tap the Edit button in the top-left corner of the Favorites screen, and a red circle with a – (minus sign) will appear before each Favorite, and on the far right of each contact, just past the type of phone number (mobile, home, etc.), you'll see **three short horizontal lines** (circled in red above). To reorder them, drag your contacts into the order you want them by tapping-and-holding on those lines and dragging your contact up or down (it's easier than it sounds). To remove a Favorite from your list, just tap directly on its red minus button, and a red Delete button will appear to its right (as seen above). Tap that **Delete button** and it's gone!

If you dial a number and you hear it ringing, but then you also hear a lower volume ring right after the regular volume ring (kind of like: RING…ring), that's telling you that the person you're calling is already on a call.

Seeing the Contact Info for a Favorite

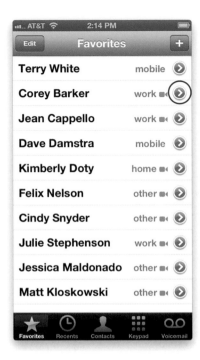

The Favorites screen is great because you can just tap the name of the contact you want to dial and the iPhone immediately begins calling that contact. However, sometimes the contact may have multiple phone numbers, such as home, work, mobile, etc., and you may not want to put every number in as a Favorite. So, the next time you need to dial a number for a Favorite contact that's not actually saved as a Favorite, bring up your Favorites list and then tap the **blue arrow button** next to the contact's name and the full Info screen appears for that contact with all the other numbers you have for them. From there, tap any one of those numbers to dial it.

Turn a Recent Caller into a Contact

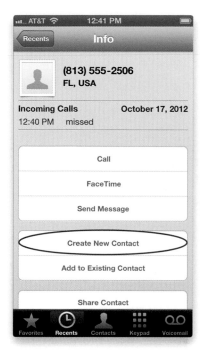

If someone calls you that isn't in your contacts list (but you'd like to add them), tap on the Phone app, then tap on Recents. Go to the number of the person you want to add as a contact, then tap on the button with the arrow in the blue circle to the right of their number. This brings up an Info screen, and near the bottom of this screen, tap the **Create New Contact button**. The New Contact screen appears with their number already entered—you just have to type in their name, address, etc. When you're done, tap the Done button in the upper-right corner of the screen. *Note:* If it's just a new number for a contact, tap the Add to Existing Contact button.

---

iTip   Adding a Note to a Contact

If you'd like to add a note to a contact (like a description of who the person is, or how you know them), tap on the contact, and when their Info screen appears, tap on the Edit button (in the top-right corner). Then, in the Info edit screen, scroll down and tap on Add Field, then scroll down and tap on Notes to add a Notes field, where you can type in your note using the keyboard that appears at the bottom of the screen.

Shooting a Photo and Adding It to a Contact

If you want to take a photo using your iPhone's camera and then add it to an existing contact, tap on the Camera app. Aim the camera and take a photo of your contact by tapping the camera shutter button at the bottom center of the screen (or press the Volume Up button on the side of your iPhone). You'll hear the shutter sound to let you know the photo has been taken. To see the photo you just took, just swipe to the right. Tap on the photo, and a row of buttons appears along the bottom of the screen. Tap the button that looks like a box with an arrow coming out of it and a menu will pop up. To assign this photo to a contact, tap the **Assign to Contact button**, and it brings up your contacts list. Tap on the contact you want to assign that photo to, and it shows you how the final photo is going to look when the contact calls, so you can move and scale it the way you want (using your finger to slide the photo around onscreen, which basically crops the photo, or "pinching it" with your fingers to scale it up or down). When it looks good to you, tap the gray Choose button and you're done.

Control the Size of Your Caller ID Photos

If you've added photos to your contacts, you may have noticed that some of them display full screen and some only display in the upper-right corner of the screen when a contact calls. This all boils down to how the photo was added to the contact. If you added the photo from your computer's address book, then it will likely display the photo small in the upper-right corner of the screen. However, if you added the photo directly on your iPhone, either using the iPhone's camera or from photos in your iPhone's Photo Library, they will display full screen when the contact calls.

---

iTip **Seeing Two Names on Your Caller ID**

You may have noticed that your caller ID display will sometimes show two names. This happens when you have two contacts in your iPhone with the same number (mine says "Scott or Kalebra Kelby" when my wife calls from home). The iPhone doesn't choose sides—it just displays both names when a call comes in from that number.

Putting a Call on Hold to Call Someone Else

If you're on a call and you want to put that person on hold while you make another call (kind of like you have a two-line phone), just tap the **Add Call button** and it automatically mutes your first call, putting the caller on hold (they can't hear you; you can't hear them), and brings up your contacts list. Now, just tap on the person's name you want to call (or, if they're not in your contacts list, tap on the Keypad button in the bottom right and just dial a number). To switch back to your original call, you can either tap the Swap button or tap the call at the top of the screen. Also, here's a tip: When you're done with the second call, don't hit the End button or it will drop both calls. Just swap to the other call. *Note:* This two-line feature may be an optional service in some areas, depending on your carrier.

Making Instant Conference Calls

To add another person to the call you're on (for a three-way call), just tap the Add Call button on the touchscreen, and it brings up your contacts list. Tap the contact's name you want added to your three-way call, then tap their number, and it dials them. Now tap the **Merge Calls button** to add them to your conversation. If the person you want added to your call isn't in your contacts list, then you can dial them by tapping on the Keypad button in the bottom-right corner of the All Contacts screen.

---

iTip | **Dialing an Extension**

*So, let's say you dial a number and you get one of those "If you know your party's extension, please dial it now" greetings. I know—how hard could it be? Actually, it's easy—if you know how. All you have to do is tap the **Keypad button** on your touchscreen, and then dial the extension. I know, it sounds really easy now, but I've seen people totally stumped when it happens to them.*

Pausing Music to Take a Call

If you've got your headset (EarPods) on and you're listening to music and a phone call comes in, you can pause the song and jump over to take the call all in one click (that's right—it's a click, not a tap). There's a little button attached to the headset (about 5" from the right EarPod itself. It doesn't look like a button, it looks like a thin little plastic rectangle). Click that button, and the song playing is paused, and it answers your call. When you're done with the call, click the button again to hang up and pick up the song right where you left off.

---

iTip **Turning Off the Call Waiting Feature**

*Call Waiting is turned on by default on your iPhone. But, if you want to turn it off, just tap on the Settings app, then tap Phone. Tap on **Call Waiting** and then tap the On/Off button to turn it off. (By the way, this only works on GSM network iPhones. If you have a CDMA network iPhone, you'll have to check with your cellular provider to find out their process for turning it off. I know, "Ugh!")*

Check Your Email While You're On the Phone

If you're in a really boring phone conversation, and you want to do what everybody else in the world does—check your email—it makes things easier if you start by tapping the Speaker button (so you can still hear your conversation while you're looking at the touch-screen). Then, press the Home button, and tap **Mail**. Don't worry—your call will stay live even though you're doing something completely different. To return to your call screen, just tap once at the very top of your screen (where it says Touch to Return to Call), and it takes you back there. *Note:* Checking your email or surfing the web while on the phone is not supported over most EDGE networks (hey, don't shoot the messenger). Also, some carriers don't support checking email or surfing the web on a cellular network while on a voice call, so you'll have to be on Wi-Fi for this to work.

How to Know If You Missed Any Calls

If you miss a call while your iPhone is asleep, when you wake it, you'll see a list of any missed calls right on the Lock screen. If you tap the icon and swipe it to the right, it will return the call. You can also see all missed calls in your iPhone's Notification Center (you can see it by simply swiping downward from the top of any screen). In fact, you'll see a list of any callers (well, you'll see their name if they're in your contacts list. If they're not, you'll just see their number and Missed Call), and if they left a voicemail, you see that listed (rather than just Missed Call), too. If you tap on a missed call, it calls that person back. If you tap on a voicemail, it takes you to that voicemail message and starts playing it. If you skip the Notification Center, then you'll see that the icon for your Phone app now has a small red circle on its top-right corner with the total number of calls you either missed or that left you a voicemail. To see those calls, tap the Phone app, then tap Recents (to see your missed calls) or tap Voicemail (to see who left you a voicemail), but you can do all that with just one downward swipe to bring up the Notification Center (it saves you time and extra taps).

Returning Missed Calls

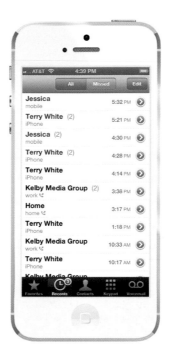

Tap on the Phone app, then tap the **Recents button** at the bottom of the screen. This brings up a list of all recent calls, and the calls you see listed in red are your missed calls. To see only your missed calls, tap the Missed button at the top. To return a missed call, just tap on it and it dials that number. (*Note*: The number of missed calls appears in a small red circle in the top-right corner of the Recents button.) If you get a call from an unfamiliar area code and number, it lists the city and state the call came from right below the number. Again, you can also return missed calls from the Notification Center by just swiping downward from the top of any screen and then tapping once on the missed call you want to return.

---

iTip   Clearing Recent Calls as a Group or Individually

*To clear all missed calls and your list of recent calls, in the Phone app, tap on Recents, tap the All button, then tap the Edit button, and a **Clear button** will appear in the top-left corner. Now, tap that Clear button and all recent and missed calls are removed. If you want to remove an individual call (missed or recent), swipe your finger sideways across the call you want to delete and a red Delete button will appear on the right side of the call listing. Tap that button to delete just that call. If you make a mistake and mark the wrong call to delete, just swipe sideways again.*

Seeing If You Have Voicemail Messages

If a caller left you a voicemail message, you'll see the caller's name (if they're in your contacts list—if not, their phone number) onscreen when you wake your iPhone from sleep or in the Notification Center when you swipe downward from the top of any screen. When you tap the green Phone app, you'll see the Voicemail button, and on it you'll see a red circle displaying the number of messages you have waiting. To see a list of your voicemails (yes, you see a list—that's why Apple calls this "Visual Voicemail"), tap on the **Voicemail button**, and you'll see a list of the contacts (or numbers) who've left you a voicemail message, and when they called. Messages with a blue dot before them haven't been listened to yet.

Listening To and Deleting Voicemail Messages

The beauty of this system is you don't have to listen to your messages in order—you can tap directly on the message you want to hear and that message plays. To hear your messages through your iPhone's speaker, tap the Speaker button on the top right. You'll see a status bar that moves from left to right as your message plays, which shows you how long the message is. Now, here's the thing: When a message is new, you just tap on it and it plays. But once you've heard it, when you tap on the message, a little blue **Play/Pause button** appears before it. To hear the message again, tap that little blue button. To pause the message, tap that same little blue button again. To return a call, tap on the message, then tap the green **Call Back button**. To delete a message, tap on it, then tap on the red **Delete button**. Once you delete a message, it's not really deleted from your iPhone—it just moves that message to a deleted area (kind of the way deleting a file on your computer just puts it in your Trash or Recycle Bin). You can still see, and hear, your deleted messages by tapping on (I know—it's pretty obvious) Deleted Messages (at the end of your voicemail list). Once there, to move a deleted message back to your regular list, just tap on it, then tap the gray Undelete button. However, if you really want all of your deleted voicemails off your iPhone for good, once you're in the Deleted screen, just tap the Clear All button. Of course, you can also play the message from the Notification Center (just swipe downward from the top of any screen to make it appear). Here, you'll see a list of any recent voicemails. To hear a voicemail, just tap on the person's name in the list (or their number), and it takes you to the Voicemail screen you see above, and automatically plays their voicemail.

Replay Just Part of a Voicemail Message

While your message is playing, you can grab the little slider and "scrub" back a few seconds and hear anything you just missed—in real time. So, for example, let's say you're listening to a message and the person on the message gives you a phone number. To hear that phone number again (without having to listen to the entire message again), you can just tap-and-hold on the little **status bar knob** and drag it back a little bit (just like you would scrub through a video), and hear it again.

Recording Your Outgoing Voicemail Message

By default, you get a generic "I'm not here, man" voicemail message, but creating your own custom message is really easy. Just tap on the Voicemail button, then in the top-left corner of the Voicemail screen, tap on the **Greeting button** to bring up the Greeting screen. You'll see two choices: (a) Default (the generic pre-recorded greeting), and (b) Custom (where you create your own). Tap on Custom, and Play and Record buttons appear at the bottom of the screen. Tap the white Record button, hold the iPhone up to your ear, and just say your message into it. When you're done, tap the red Stop button, and to hear it, tap the blue Play button. If you don't like your message, just tap the white Record button again and record a new message. When it sounds good to you, tap the Save button in the upper-right corner of the screen.

Setting Up Call Forwarding

Tap on the Settings app, then in the Settings screen, tap on Phone. In the Phone settings screen, tap on **Call Forwarding** and you'll see an ON/OFF button (by default, it's off). To turn it on, tap this button. Now, you're probably wondering where your call is forwarded to. Once you turn on the Call Forwarding feature, if you don't already have a Forwarding To number entered, you'll see a screen where you enter that phone number. Now, this next part throws a lot of people: there's no OK or Save button. You just have to tap the Call Forwarding button in the top-left corner and it returns you to the main Call Forwarding screen, where you'll see the number you just added and the ON setting. When you want to turn the Call Forwarding feature off, go back to the same screen, and tap the ON button, and it will change to OFF. (*Note:* This applies to AT&T's network. Other networks may require you to make the changes online, with a link under the network's services in the Phone settings.)

---

iTip **Turning On Do Not Disturb**

Do Not Disturb keeps any calls, texts, alerts, or vibrating sounds from coming through any time this feature is turned on (like while you're sleeping), but best of all, you can set which times you want it to be turned on automatically. For details about setting this up, see Chapter 14.

Can't Take a Call Now? Reply with a Text Message

If a call comes in, but you can't take it right now, just swipe upward on the little phone icon at the bottom right of the screen (next to the Answer button) and tap the **Reply with Message button**. By default, there are three text messages pre-written for you. They are: (1) "Can't talk right now…I'll call you later," (2) "Can't talk right now…I'm on my way," and (3) "Can't talk right now…I have a festering boil that's just about to pop." (Okay, I made up that last one, but it's something like that.) Anyway, to send one of those pre-written texts to the person calling you, just tap on its button. The good news is, though, that you don't have to use those pre-written texts (although, #3 is tempting)—you can customize them. Start by tapping on the Settings app, then tap on Phone, and then tap on **Reply with Message**. You'll see the three default text messages, but you can just tap on any of them and type in your own (I would at least consider, "Can't talk right now…I'm arranging bail."). If you're okay with leaving the default pre-written messages, you can still send your own custom reply that you enter right when the call comes in—just flick upward and at the bottom of the list of text replies, tap the Custom button, and type in your own for just that call.

Get Reminded Later That You Didn't Take That Call

If you can't take a call right now, but want to be sure you don't forget to call that person back, you can use the Remind Me Later feature. When your iPhone rings, just swipe upward on the little phone icon on the bottom right of the screen (next to the Answer button) and then tap on the **Remind Me Later button**. A pop-up menu appears with four choices: (1) In 1 hour, (2) When I leave, (3) When I get home, and (4) When I get to work. So, how does it know when you leave or when you get to work or home? Well, for the leaving/arriving ones, it uses your iPhone's built-in Location Services. So, for example, when you leave the restaurant you're having lunch in, your phone's built-in GPS knows you left that location and that triggers you getting an onscreen reminder (pretty clever, right?). As for knowing when you get to work or home, it uses Location Services and the Home and Work addresses you added in the Contacts app for your name (so make sure you enter both of those, and not just your phone number).

---

iTip What to Do If Remind Me Later Only Shows In 1 Hour Button

*If you only see the In 1 Hour button when you choose Remind Me Later, that's probably because you have Location Services turned off in your Reminders app. Tap on the Settings app, then tap on Privacy, then tap **Location Services**. Scroll down to Reminders and make sure it's set to On. Now, you'll have all four choices.*

Adding a Pause

If you're calling a number and you need to enter an extension (account number, PIN, etc.), you can add those pauses and additional numbers directly to your contact's Info screen. Tap on the Phone app, then tap on Contacts to bring up your contacts list. Tap on the contact that needs the additional string of numbers and pauses. Tap the Edit button in the top right of the screen, tap on the phone number that you need to edit, and tap the symbol key (+*#) at the bottom left of the keyboard. This will change the 4 key to a Pause key. Now you can tap the **Pause key** to enter a two-second pause, and then type the next string of numbers. If you need a longer pause, just continue to tap the Pause key for as many two-second pauses as you need. You can also add a hard pause by tapping the **Wait key**. This causes the iPhone to pause and wait until you tap the Dial button to send the numbers. Once you're done, tap Done at the top right of the screen to save the number and the contact's changes.

Turning the Ringer Off

If you don't want to hear your iPhone's ringer at all, tap on the Settings app. In the Settings screen, tap on Sounds, then in the Ringer and Alerts section, tap-and-drag the **volume slider** all the way to the left. This turns your ring volume off. Your phone will still vibrate when a call comes in, but there won't be an audible ring. If you want to turn that vibration off, as well, in the Vibrate section at the top, turn **Vibrate on Ring** off by tapping on its ON/OFF button. You can also turn the ringer off by moving the **Ring/Silent switch** (found on the top-left side of the iPhone) toward the back of the iPhone to Silent mode. And, if you want to turn the vibration off when it's in Silent mode, just turn Vibrate on Silent off.

iTip **Stop the Ringing**

*If a call comes in, and you can't take it right then, but don't want the phone to continue ringing, then just press the **Sleep/Wake button** on the top of the iPhone. This stops the ringing and sends the call into your voicemail.*

Choosing Your Ringtone

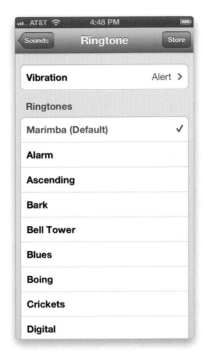

The default ringtone for your iPhone is a marimba sound, but if you'd like to change it, tap on the Settings app. In the Settings screen, tap on Sounds, then in the Sounds and Vibration Patterns section, tap on **Ringtone**, and it takes you to a screen listing all the built-in ringtones and any custom ringtones you've synced to your iPhone. You'll see a checkmark to the right of Marimba, telling you that it's the current ringtone. To change it, tap on the name of the one you want. That ringtone plays (so you can hear if you really want to select it), and if you want to keep this new sound as your ringtone, just leave that screen (tap the Sounds button in the top-left corner of the Ringtone screen, or press the Home button).

Assigning Ringtones to Specific Callers

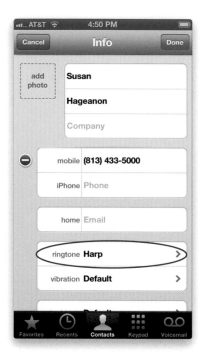

If you'd like to assign a specific ringtone to a contact (for example, I have a ringtone assigned to my wife's cell phone number, so I instantly know it's her without even looking at my phone), here's what to do: Tap on the Phone app, then tap the Contacts button. Tap on the contact you want to assign a ringtone to, then when their Info screen appears, tap the Edit button in the top right, then tap on Default (next to Ringtone), and you'll be taken to the Ringtone screen. To assign a ringtone to this contact, just tap on one (it will play a sample of the ringtone when you tap on it). When you find the one you want, just tap the Save button at the top right of the screen, and it returns you to the contact's Info screen, where you'll see the name of the ringtone you just assigned in the Ringtone field. Tap the Done button, and now when this contact calls, you'll hear their custom ringtone rather than the default ringtone that you'll hear when anyone else calls.

---

iTip   Stop People You Call from Seeing Your Number

*If you want to call somebody, but you'd prefer that they not see your number, tap on the Settings app. Scroll down and tap on Phone, and then tap on **Show My Caller ID** to bring up that screen with an ON/OFF button. Just tap that button to switch this feature off. (Note: This applies to AT&T's network. Other networks may require you to make the changes online, with a link under the network's services in the Phone settings.)*

Headsets or Bluetooth in Your Car

If you have a Bluetooth wireless headset, or you want to pair your iPhone to your car's Bluetooth feature, here's what to do: First you have to put your headset (or your car's Bluetooth feature) in Discoverable mode, which means you put it in a mode where other Bluetooth devices can find it. How this is done is different for every headset or car make and model, so look at your headset's instruction manual (or your car's owner's manual) for how to make it "discoverable." Once it's discoverable, tap on the Settings app, then tap on **Bluetooth**. When the Bluetooth screen appears, tap the ON/OFF button to turn the Bluetooth feature on. This starts your iPhone searching for any discoverable Bluetooth devices (like your wireless headset or your car's Bluetooth feature) that are within about 30 feet of where you are. Once it finds a Bluetooth device, it displays that device's name. Tap the Not Paired button, which will bring up a screen where you enter the PIN for your device (check the instructions that come with your headset or car kit for how to find this information), then tap Pair, and they'll be paired (luckily, you only have to go through this process the first time. After that, it automatically recognizes your headset, or car).

Set Up to Make FaceTime Video Calls

To make a FaceTime video call, first you need to make sure both people on the call have an iPhone 5, 4S, or 4 (you can't make video calls with an iPhone 3GS, because it doesn't have a camera on the front of it), or a Mac, or another iOS device that supports FaceTime. You also need to be on a Wi-Fi network (so, for me, this means I can make FaceTime calls any time I'm at the office, or at home, or at a Wi-Fi hotspot) or, if you have an iPhone 5 or 4S, you can use a cellular data connection (you set this up through your provider). If you've got both of these covered, then you'll just need to make sure the FaceTime feature is on (you only have to do this the first time, unless you turn it off later). Tap on the Settings app, scroll down and tap on FaceTime, and then turn **FaceTime** on by tapping the ON/OFF button. Now your iPhone is all set to make FaceTime video calls. By the way, since FaceTime is essentially an Internet video call, it doesn't use up your cellular phone minutes if you use it over Wi-Fi. (How cool is that?)

Making a FaceTime Video Call

Now that you've got your iPhone set up to make FaceTime video calls, there are four different ways to make one:

(1) Tap on the Phone app, and then tap on Contacts to find the person you want to have a FaceTime video call with. When you get to their Info screen, tap the **FaceTime button** (as shown circled above left). If you have more than one phone number or email address for this person (like home, mobile, etc.), it will bring up a list of them. Just tap the one you want (remember to call their iOS device), and it makes the FaceTime call.

(2) You can make a regular phone call using the Phone app, and once the person answers, you can tap the **FaceTime button** (shown circled above right) to switch to a video call.

(3) If you recently had a FaceTime video call with someone, if you tap on the Phone app, then tap the **Recents button**, you'll see their name (or number) on this screen, along with a video camera icon. If you tap on their name to call them, it redials as a FaceTime call.

(4) If you want to have a FaceTime video call with someone who doesn't have an iPhone (they have an iPad mini, an iPad with Retina display, an iPad 2, or an iPod touch), then you'll need to choose their FaceTime email address instead to start the FaceTime call.

Whichever method you choose, the person you're calling will have to accept your FaceTime call invitation. Once they tap **Accept**, your video call begins.

During Your FaceTime Call

The camera on the front of the phone turns on first to show you a preview of how you'll look to the person on the other end. Once they accept your call, your image shrinks down to a small thumbnail up in the top-right corner of your screen (like a TV picture-in-picture view), and their video image fills your screen. You talk just like you're using the speakerphone feature. If you need to pause the video part of your call (but keep the speakerphone live), press the Home button (this is handy if you need to look up something in another app). To return to video, tap the green bar at the top. To mute your mic, tap the Mute icon in the bottom left. Normally, the person you're having a FaceTime call with will see you during the call, but if you want, you can switch to the camera on the back of your iPhone, so they see whatever you point your camera at, by tapping the Camera Swap icon in the bottom-right corner (the camera with the circular arrow around it). The tiny thumbnail in the top-right corner now shows the camera's view on the back of your iPhone, so you can see what they're seeing. Also, just rotate your iPhone sideways to get a wider shot. To switch back, press the same Camera Swap icon. To end the call, tap the End button.

---

iTip   You Can Move the Tiny Thumbnail Preview Window

Once you start a FaceTime video call, what your camera is showing shrinks down to a small thumbnail preview in the upper-right corner. If it's blocking something you want to see, move it by tapping-and-holding on it, then dragging it to a different corner.

Use FaceTime and Not Cellular Minutes

One of the hidden treasures in the iPhone's FaceTime feature is that it works over Wi-Fi. This means that since you and the person you're talking to each have an iPhone 5, 4S, or 4 (or another compatible iOS device) and are on a Wi-Fi network, you can make unlimited FaceTime calls without ever using any cellular minutes. This is great for international travel or any other situation where roaming would be expensive.

Chapter Three
Message in a Bottle
Sending Text Messages

"Message in a Bottle" (by The Sheriffs) is a better name than it first sounds, because there is nothing in your iPhone that says "Texting." Nope. Instead, you send texts using an app called Messages. Now, I know what you're thinking, "Wouldn't an app named Messages be where you go to check your voicemail messages?" Nope, that's called Voicemail (which is in the Phone app). So, couldn't they just have called the app "Texting" or "Text?" Sure. Could you just call The Police (who did "Message in a Bottle") The Sheriffs, since they pretty much do the same thing? Ahh, see, this is why this is all so sticky, but in the secret world of app naming, the person who names the app the furthest from what it actually does gets a huge bonus at the end of the year (along with a large trophy they hold above their head as they skate around the rink). Anyway, in this case, Messages isn't a bad name, because it's half of the phrase "Text Messages," so the person that named this app won't be skating around with the trophy anytime soon. Neither will the person who named the Stocks, Weather, Camera, Photos, Maps, Calendar, Mail, Phone, or Clock apps. In fact, I'm not sure if anybody at Apple will be up for the award this year, because it all makes too much sense. Ya know, Microsoft has their own Windows phone out now, but of course their corporate slogan is "Making simple everyday things just that much harder," and although I haven't actually used a Windows phone (in fact, I'm not sure really anyone has), I imagine their apps are named in a very Microsoft-like way. For example, I would guess that their texting app would probably be called something like "Bing XP," and their phone app would be something like "Excel Chart," and their calendar app would probably be called "Office Bing." Hey, I heard that the original name for the Windows phone was supposed to be "Zune iBing Vista Maintenance Pack 4a.10B."

Sending Text Messages

Tap on the Messages app, then tap on the button with a square with a pencil in it (in the upper-right corner of the screen), which brings up the New Message screen. At the top, you type your contact's name, and as soon as you start to type, it searches for the name in your contacts list. If they're not in your contacts list, just type in their phone number. Now, tap once in the field above the keyboard, type in your text message, then tap the green **Send button**. Your messages appear in green bubbles, replies will appear in gray bubbles, and visually it looks like you're having a conversation. If you're sending a text message to someone else who has an iPhone, then your Send button and message will appear in blue (more on this feature, called "iMessage," on page 57).

Sending Messages to Multiple People

It's possible to send the same text or picture message to two or more people at once. Launch Messages and tap the button with a square with a pencil in it in the top right. Start typing in the name of the first person (or phone number, if they're not in your contacts list), and tap their name if it comes up in the search results below the To field (or if you typed in their phone number, tap in the message field, then tap back into the To field), then type in another name or number for another person you want to send the message to. You can also tap the + (plus sign) button to add contacts directly from your contacts list. Now, in the past, if you sent a message to two or more people, when they responded, each person's response would start a new one-on-one individual text thread between you and just that person. But, in iOS 5 and later, if you have **Group Messaging** turned on in the Messages settings in the Settings app, when someone responds, they automatically respond to all the other recipients, as well—kind of like a group conversation.

Seeing If You Have Text Messages

When a text message comes in, the sender's name and the first line of their text message appear right at the top of your screen for a few seconds, as shown above left (of course, if you don't have their name in your contacts list, you'll only see their phone number and not their name). If your iPhone is asleep when their text message comes in, then when you wake it, you'll see their message on the Lock screen. If you have more than one new message, you can swipe downward to see all of them listed at the top of the Lock screen (shown above right), and to see the text of any message in the list, just unlock your phone. If you look at the Messages app icon on the Home screen, you'll see it keeps track of how many unread messages you have, by showing that number in a little red circle on the top-right corner of the icon (so, if you see a 4 in a red circle, that means you have four unread messages).

---

iTip **Seeing Which Text Messages Haven't Been Read Yet**

If you see a number on the Messages app icon, tap on it, and the messages in the list with a blue dot beside them are the ones you haven't read yet.

iMessage: Send Unlimited Free Texts! Really!

iMessage is a very cool texting feature (built into the Messages app) that lets you send texts to other iOS users (iPhone, iPad, iPod touch) or Mac users running OSX Mountain Lion via Wi-Fi, 3G, or LTE (iPhone 5 only), rather than using your phone's data plan, so you don't get charged standard messaging rates (you don't get charged at all). To start, tap the Settings app, then tap on Messages, and turn on **iMessage** (as shown above left). Now, you have free unlimited texting as long as: (a) you have a Wi-Fi, 3G, or LTE connection *and* (b) you're sending your text to another device that is using iOS 5 or newer (or Mountain Lion), and that has iMessage turned on, too. If your text is sent as an iMessage, two things happen: (1) you'll see the word iMessage appear right above your text conversation (as shown circled above right), and (2) your text message will now appear in a blue talk bubble. To send iMessages to friends who are using an iPod touch, an iPad (any iOS 5 or newer device) or a Mac, you just need their Apple ID (and, of course, they need to have iMessage turned on and an Internet connection).

> **iTip** **Another iMessage Advantage Is You'll See When They Start Typing**
>
> *When you text with iMessage, as soon as the person you're texting with starts to reply to your text, you'll see a little talk bubble with three little dots appear on their side of the conversation, letting you know that they're working on their response. You'll miss this when you're not using iMessage, because it's really amazingly handy.*

How to Know If You're Sending an iMessage

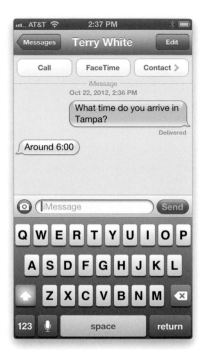

One way to tell if the person you're about to text will receive your text as an iMessage (meaning, you're using free unlimited texting to this person) is to look at the color of the Send button for your text. If the button is blue, you're sending a free iMessage. If it's green, you're using regular texting (and you're paying. Well, you're probably paying—it just depends on your texting plan, but you know what I mean). Once you've started texting, another visual reminder is the color of your talk bubble. If you're using iMessage, it's blue. If not, it's green. Green means "Go!" as in "Go talk them into getting an iPhone, so your text messaging to them is free (it'll be free for them, too!)."

---

iTip   Your iPhone Knows If You're Texting Another iPhone

You don't have to worry about managing iMessage—your iPhone automatically detects when you're texting somebody else with an iPhone and, if they have iMessage turned on, then it automatically sends your messages back and forth using iMessage.

Deleting Individual Messages

If you want to delete an individual text message from your conversation, just tap the Edit button in the top-right corner of the message screen, then tap right on the text you want to delete. This adds a red checkmark beside the comment, letting you know that's the one you've marked to be deleted (if you want to delete other comments, tap on those, too). Now, just tap the red **Delete button** on the bottom left of the screen. If you change your mind, just tap on the text again.

---

iTip   Deleting Entire Conversations

*If you want to delete an entire text conversation (as if it never happened), go to that conversation, tap the Edit button up top, then tap the **Clear All button** that appears at the top left of the screen. There's also a shortcut: in your list of messages, just swipe sideways over the message, and a red **Delete button** will appear. Tap it, and it's gone.*

Forwarding Individual Messages

Tap on the Messages app and go to the particular message that you want to forward all or part of. Tap the **Edit button** in the upper-right corner of the screen and you'll see circles appear next to each response in the message. You can select one or more of them by tapping on their talk bubbles, and then you can forward them to someone else by tapping the Forward button at the bottom of the screen. This brings up a New Message screen with the responses you selected already in the message field. Just type in a contact or phone number to send it to, and tap Send.

---

iTip   Calling a Phone Number You've Been Texted

If someone texts you a phone number, you'll notice it's underlined in blue. That's because your iPhone recognizes that it's a phone number, and that blue underline means it's a "live link." So, if you tap on that number, it dials it for you. Sweet!

If Your Text Doesn't Go Through

You'll see a little red alert exclamation point appear to the right of the message (this will usually only happen if you're in an area with really bad cell reception). To have it try to resend the text message, just tap on the exclamation point icon, then tap the **Try Again button**. If it's successful, the message will appear in a bubble just like always and the exclamation point icon will be gone. Otherwise, it will stay there in the bubble with the red warning beside it. Also, if you tap the Send button, and then switch to another app (thinking your message was sent with no problem), the Messages app will try to alert you that the message didn't go by adding a red exclamation point warning to the Messages app's icon (as shown above right).

---

iTip If Your iMessage Doesn't Go Through

If you send an iMessage, but it seems to have stalled (probably due to bad reception coverage), you can send the message via cellular text messaging by just tapping-and-holding on the message, and if it hasn't been delivered yet, you can choose to send it as a text message instead. Also, if the message does fail, you'll be given the choice to send it as a text message, or it will eventually just send it as one, but with this tip you don't have to wait for it to time out/fail.

Sending Photos or Videos in a Text Message

Go to Messages and tap the button with a square with a pencil in it in the top right. Now, type in the name or phone number of the person you're texting, then tap the **Attach Media button** to the left of the message field (the camera icon). A menu pops up asking if you want to take a photo or video or choose one already on your iPhone. If you tap Take Photo or Video, it takes you to the Camera app to take your photo (or video). Once you take it, you'll see a preview of it. If you don't like it, tap the Retake button to try again. If you like it, tap the Use button, and it attaches that photo (or video) to a text message (and automatically com-presses the size of it). If you tapped the Choose Existing button instead, it takes you to your photo albums, where you can choose a photo (or video) in any album by just tapping on it. It shows you a preview of the photo (or video), and if it looks good, tap the Choose button (if not, tap Cancel). It'll appear in the text field, and now just tap the Send button. Also, if you choose a photo (or video) to send, but before you send it, you change your mind, just hit the Backspace key (on the keyboard) a few times to delete it. If someone sends you a photo or video, it appears in a text bubble, just like text. To see it larger, tap directly on it.

---

iTip **Turning On MMS Messaging**

*If, for some reason, the ability to send MMS (photo and video) messages isn't turned on, tap on the Settings app, then tap on Messages. Tap the **MMS Messaging ON/OFF button** to turn it on.*

Video Quality and Text (MMS) Messaging

Video files are much, much larger in file size than photos, so your iPhone has to greatly compress and shrink your video clip's physical size, so it's small enough to be delivered as an MMS message. Because of that, the quality of the video you're sending isn't quite as good as the original video you shot. It will probably look a little pixelated and generally a bit lower in quality than how it looked after you viewed it on your own iPhone. So, if keeping the original video quality intact is really important to you, then instead of sending the video as a text message, email it, and it will look a lot better.

---

iTip   Seeing More Messages

*When you look at the list of text conversations you've had with a particular person, it only displays the last 55 texts between you two. So, if you need to find texts previous to those 55, from the top of the message list, tap on **Load Earlier Messages**, and it will load the next earlier batch.*

Sending Voice Memos in a Text Message

If you've recorded a voice memo, you can send that in a text message. Start in the Voice Memos app (in the Utilities folder), then tap on the button to the right of the VU meter to see a list of your voice memos. Tap on the voice memo you want to send, then tap the blue Share button at the bottom left. A menu will pop up; tap **Message** and it attaches that voice memo to a new, blank text message. Now just type in the recipient's name (or phone number), and then tap the Send button. If you want to add any text along with your voice memo, just tap once on the message field, and type in your message.

---

iTip Searching Through Your Text Messages

*If there's a particular message you're trying to find, you can search by any word in the text. So, if you were talking about pizza delivery, you could search for the word "pizza" by using the **Search field** at the top of the Messages screen.*

Use Siri to Do Your Texting for You

If you don't want to type your texts (maybe you're driving), then just let Siri type and send your texts for you. Say, "Send a text to [the person's name]," then Siri will say she can send a text to [the person's name] and ask what you'd like it to say. Now, if Siri gets the name wrong or doesn't understand you, she will let you know and guess which of your contacts' names you said. If she's right, say, "Yes," and she will then ask you what you want to say. Just say your message (don't speak really fast, of course). When you're done, pause for a couple of seconds and Siri will show your message, and then ask if you're "ready to send it." Just say "Yes," and off it goes, all without you touching your keyboard. Learn more about Siri in Chapter 8.

Other Ways to Text Your Contacts

There are a couple of other places where you can directly text from, rather than having to go to the Home screen and tap Messages every time. For example, if you're looking at a contact in the Contacts app, you'll see a button there for **Send Message**. Tap it, choose the phone number or email to send it to, and it takes you to the New Message screen with that person's name already entered for you. If you want to text the person you're currently talking with on the phone (I use this to text the person a phone number we talked about, without them having to write it down), in the Phone app, tap on Contacts, tap on the person's name you're talking to, then tap the Send Message button. If you're looking at a Voicemail message instead, and want to text the person who left you the voice message, tap the **blue arrow button** to the right of the voice message, then tap the Send Message button.

---

iTip **Turning Off the Pop-Up Previews**

If you'd rather not see the pop-up onscreen text message previews, tap on the Settings app, then tap Notifications. Under In Notification Center, tap on Messages, and turn off **Show Preview***.*

Turning Off the "You've Got a Text Message" Sound

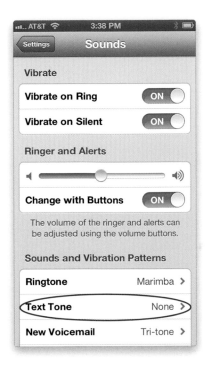

By default, when you get a text message, you get an alert sound that lets you know it's there (if your iPhone's Ring/Silent switch isn't set to Silent, of course). If you'd rather not get an alert sound each time a text message comes in, you can turn it off by tapping on the Settings app, then tapping on Sounds, then tapping on **Text Tone** and it displays the sounds you can choose as your alert (by default, it's set to Tri-tone). To turn off the alert sound, just tap on None at the top. By default, it's also set to vibrate when you get a text, so if you want to turn this off, as well, tap on **Vibration** at the top of the Text Tone screen and then tap on None at the bottom. Now tap the Home button to close Settings.

---

iTip   **Your iPhone Will Alert You**

*When you receive a message, your iPhone will sound an alert (provided you have that preference set in your Sounds settings). However, you may be away from your iPhone or unable to hear it in a noisy environment, so you can set it to repeat that alert: in the Settings app, tap on Notifications, then tap on Messages, and tap on **Repeat Alert**.*

Seeing How Many Characters You've Typed

If you're typing a really long text message, your iPhone will tell you how many characters you've typed. You'll want to know this because there's a 160-character limit for a single SMS text (this does not apply to iMessage, which does not have a limit). To turn on this feature, tap on the Settings app, then tap on Messages, and then tap the **Character Count ON/OFF button** to turn it on. Now, once you type more than 50 characters, a little character counter automatically appears next to the top-right corner of the message field, showing you how many characters you've typed.

Create Your Own Keyboard Shortcuts for Texting

If you're like me and wind up sending the same short text message fairly often (my favorite is "Running 10 minutes late"), you can add these as shortcuts, so you only have to type a few letters and it types in the full message for you. To create your own text shortcuts, tap on the Settings app, then tap on General, scroll down, and tap on Keyboard. At the bottom of the Keyboard settings, you'll see a Shortcuts section (as seen above on the left). To create your own custom shortcut, tap the **Add New Shortcut button**, then type in the phrase (maybe something like "I'm driving---I'll text back in a few minutes"), then type the shortcut you want (maybe "drv"), then tap the blue Save button at the top right. Now when you type "drv," you'll see a little pop-up message displaying "I'm driving---I'll text back in a few minutes." If that's what you want to say, just tap the spacebar and it fills in the rest for you. Feel free to add as many shortcuts as you'd like (of course, now you have a new challenge— remembering all your shortcuts).

---

iTip **Have Your iPhone Flash Its Flash When You Get a Text Message**

*You can actually set your iPhone up so the LED flash for your camera will flash when you get a text message. Tap on the Settings app, then tap on General. Now, scroll down to Accessibility and turn on **LED Flash for Alerts**. That's it. Now when your iPhone's asleep and people text you, you'll visually see a flashing light. What happens if you're in a nightclub and someone texts you? Sadly, you'll never know.*

Productivity

 Contacts

 Calendar

 Notes

 Passbook

 Evernote

 Errands

 Voice Memos

 eFax

 FedEx Mobile

 Dropbox

 Safari

 Adobe Reader

 CMPro Lite

 iTranslate

 Wi-Fi Finder

 Quick Scan

Chapter Four
App Anthem
Using Apps & the App Store

 Believe it or not, I actually could have gone with the name "APP" or "A.P.P." for the name of this chapter, because apparently we have run out of decent names for bands and songs. APP is a band that has one song in the iTunes Store, "I'm on Fire," which is a cover of Bruce Springsteen's "I'm on Fire." I looked at the popularity ranking for "I'm on Fire" by APP, and it clearly was not, so then I looked at a song called "A.P.P." by a band called Papa Project, and it sounded like a harmless reggae-style background track, but I was afraid of what A.P.P. might actually stand for, so I went with a safer bet: "App Anthem," by Jimmy Towle/Doug Kaufman. "App Anthem" is actually a pretty decent sounding rap tune, and while it's certainly possible "App Anthem" may be littered with dirty words, I'll never know, because I couldn't make out a single word, but I don't feel bad because I'm pretty sure no one older than 14 has even a remote chance of deciphering them. In fact, I doubt that decryption experts at the CIA could figure out what's actually being said in your average rap song, which makes you wonder why other countries don't just have secret messages sent to their embedded field operatives via rap tunes. Think about it—the only way we'd be able to crack the code is if we were able to convince a 14-year-old to stop playing *Halo* long enough to write down what's being said. But, 14-year-olds don't write anymore, they text, and they use a shorthand for texting that only other 14-year-olds can possibly understand, and honestly, it would be easier for us to just to do the old "briefcase switcharoo" routine than it would be to find a 14-year-old that hasn't already been hired by the breakaway Republic of Irapistan. I miss the old days when we just used invisible ink.

Downloading iPhone Apps to Your Computer

There are two places to buy apps (short for "applications") for your iPhone: the first one is on your computer through Apple's iTunes Store (iTunes comes on every Mac, and is available for free download for Windows PCs at Apple.com). You download the apps onto your computer, and then when you sync your iPhone to your computer, it uploads the apps to your iPhone (if you have that preference set). To get to the App Store on your computer, launch iTunes, then click on the iTunes Store link in the Source list on the left. Next, click on Apps at the top of the iTunes Store's homepage, and you'll see featured apps, lists of the most popular apps, and, of course, you can search for apps using the Search Store field at the top right of the window, just like you do for songs or videos. Once you find an app that you want to download and use, you can click on it and then click the **Buy App button** (or the **Free App button**, if it's free). Your apps will be downloaded to your computer, ready to sync to your iPhone.

iTip Only Pay for Apps Once

If you buy an app and then, for whatever reason, you delete it later, you can always redownload/re-install the apps you get from the App Store without paying for them again. They are tied to your Apple ID, and Apple knows which ones you've downloaded.

Getting Apps from Your iPhone's App Store

You can also download apps wirelessly from your iPhone's App Store. Just tap on the App Store app and you'll be connected to the same App Store as if you were doing it via iTunes, however, this App Store is formatted specifically for your iPhone. You can browse the New and Noteworthy or What's Hot Featured apps, or you can look through the Paid, Free, and Top Grossing Charts, as well as Categories, or check out the apps recommended by Genius. If you know the name of the app you're looking for, you can tap Search and type the name of the app to search for it. You can also use the Genius feature here (more on using this with music in Chapter 10). Once you find an app you want to download to your iPhone, tap on it, then just tap the price (or Free) button, then tap the **Buy Now (or Install App) button**, and you'll be asked to enter your Apple ID username and password. The app will be downloaded and installed directly on your iPhone. The next time you sync your iPhone with your computer, the app will be downloaded to your iTunes Apps Library for backup (if you have that preference set).

---

iTip **Downloading Apps That Are Larger Than 20MB**

Although you can download most apps using your iPhone's cellular data network, if a particular app you want to download is larger than 20MB in size, you'll have to jump on a Wi-Fi network to download this large a file.

Deleting Apps

Although you can't delete the apps put on your iPhone by Apple, you can easily delete apps that you've downloaded from the App Store. On the Home screen, tap-and-hold your finger on the app you want to remove. All of your icons will start to wiggle and you'll see an X appear in the upper-left corner of each app you downloaded from the App Store. Tap the **X** to remove the app from your iPhone. The next time you sync your iPhone, the app will also be removed from iTunes (if you have that preference set).

iTip   **Viewing Your iTunes Store Account Info**

*If you want to view or change your iTunes Store account info, you can do that right from your iPhone. Tap on the Settings app, then scroll down to iTunes & App Stores. Now, enter your Apple ID info, tap on Sign In, and you'll have access to your account info by tapping on your Apple ID and then tapping on **View Apple ID**. You can change your payment method, or even sign up to receive the store newsletter or special offers.*

Updating Your Apps

App developers are constantly updating their apps with new features, improvements, and bug fixes, and most of these updates are absolutely free. Just tap on the App Store app and you'll see an Updates button in the lower-right corner with the number of apps on your iPhone that have had updates released appearing in a small red circle (as seen above). Tap on it to see your list of apps that have updates, and to see what features (or fixes) have been included in an update, tap on it, then scroll down to the What's New section. To download the update, just tap the **Update button** at the top of the update's Info screen. If you have multiple apps that have updates, you can download all of them at once by tapping Update All at the top right of the Updates screen.

Quickly Switching to Another App

iOS 5 and later support multitasking, as well as fast app switching. If an app supports either of these technologies, you'll be able to toggle back and forth between multiple apps without having to close one and return to the Home screen first. Just double-click the Home button and the multitasking bar will appear at the bottom of the screen. Tap on the app you want to switch to and it will open. By default, you'll see the last four apps you used in the multitasking bar. However, you can scroll the bar to the right to see more.

Rearranging Your Apps

To move an app to a different location, just tap-and hold on any one for a few seconds until all the icons start to wiggle. Now, tap-and-drag the icon of the app you want to move to a new location (the other apps will move aside to make room for the app you're moving). If you want to drag your app to a different screen (you can have multiple screens of apps), just drag the app to the right or left edge of the screen until the next screen appears. You can either release the icon there or drag it to the edge again to advance to the next screen, and so on. When you're done moving apps around, just press the Home button to lock in your changes.

Cut the App Clutter by Creating Folders

It doesn't take long before you've downloaded a lot of apps (they're kind of addictive), and pretty soon you've got screen after screen of apps, and you spend a lot of time scrolling through them. To keep things organized, you can use folders (just like you do on your computer). That way, you can have a folder of games, or a folder of photo apps, or shopping apps, sports apps, and so on. To create a folder, start by tapping-and-holding on an app until the icons all start wiggling. Now, just drag that app onto a similar app (for example, if you wanted to create a folder of movie apps, maybe you'd tap on Movies by Flixster [my favorite movie app] and drag it on top of AMC Theatres), and the two now appear in a folder. You can drag other similar apps into this folder (you can have up to a total of 16 apps per folder). By the way, your iPhone tries to help you out by applying a name to your folder based on the first app you dragged in there, so if you dragged Movies by Flixster onto the AMC Theatres app, it would automatically name the folder "Entertainment," but you can just type a different name in the name field if you'd like (I changed it to "Movies"). To remove an app from a folder, while the icons are wiggling, just tap on it and drag it right out of the folder. When you're done creating folders (and moving apps in and out of these folders), press the Home button to lock in your changes.

Access More Apps at the Bottom of Your Screen

You know those four apps at the bottom of the screen that are always there, no matter which Home screen you're on? Those apps are in the Dock, and it's there so you can have quick access to four of your most-used apps. By default, Apple placed four apps there that they thought you would want to have available at all times, like the Phone app (that makes sense, right!). But, what if you want more than just four apps in your Dock? Then use this trick: create a folder of your other most-used apps (up to 16 different apps), then drag that folder down to the Dock to replace one of those four that maybe you don't use very often. Now you have a total of 19 apps in your Dock (three regular apps and your new folder full of apps) that you can quickly get to no matter which Home screen you happen to be on. Of course, you could replace all four of the apps in the Dock with folders, and then you'd have 64 apps down there, visible all the time (but I would still leave at least the Phone app by itself, but hey, that's just me).

---

iTip **Moving Between Home Screens**

Since you can add web clips and apps to the Home screen, the iPhone gives you up to 11 Home screens. Once you have two or more Home screens, you will see little dots above the Dock indicating how many Home screens you have, and which screen you're looking at (its dot appears white). You can either tap a dot to switch screens or you can flick the screens left or right like you do with pictures.

Don't Miss Apple's Own Downloadable Apps

Your iPhone comes with a number of Apple-designed apps already pre-installed (like Contacts, Stocks, Weather, and so on), but there are a number of really handy, very clever Apple apps that aren't pre-installed that you can get from the App Store. When you get to the App Store, tap on Search and simply type "Apple." When the results appear, you'll find some great apps like Find My iPhone, Find My Friends, Remote (for controlling your Apple TV or your Mac), the Apple Store app (for buying Apple-related hardware and accessories), Podcasts (for downloading and playing podcasts), iTunes U (for downloading educational content), iBooks (for downloading and reading books), iTunes Movie Trailers, and Cards (for creating printed postcards), which are all free. There are also Apple apps you can buy, like GarageBand (for creating music), iPhoto (for managing photos), Numbers (a spreadsheet app), Keynote (for slide presentations), Pages (a word processor), and iMovie (for creating movies).

Accessing Your Audio Controls While in Another App

Once you have music going in your Music app or any third-party audio app, like Pandora Radio, you can launch another app and the music will keep playing. However, if you want to control the music, you don't have to go back to the app to do this. You can access the controls widget by double-clicking the Home button and scrolling to the left in the multitasking bar at the bottom of the screen.

Organizing Your iPhone Apps on Your Computer

While it's great that I can rearrange my apps and make folders right on my iPhone (see page 78 for more on making folders), when I have a lot of arranging to do, I prefer to do it on my computer in iTunes. iTunes lets you rearrange the order of the apps on your Home screens (as shown above), as well as the Home screens themselves (on the right side of the window), just by clicking-and-dragging. So, if you have a lot of arranging to do, just connect your iPhone to your computer and select it in the iTunes Source list. Click on the **Apps tab** and you can choose which apps to sync, as well as click-and-drag them into the order you want, create new app folders (just like you would on your iPhone), or hover your cursor over an app and click on the X button at the top left to delete it. Once you're done, click the Sync button to sync your iPhone. You can also check in iTunes to see if your apps have any available updates: just click on your Apps Library in the Source list on the left side of the iTunes window. Then, click the **Check for Updates link** in the bottom-right corner of the window (or the link that tells you how many updates are available), and if there are any updates available, you'll be taken to a screen that lists them, and where you can update them individually or all at once.

Where to Find the Very Coolest Apps

There are literally hundreds of thousands of apps in the iTunes App Store, and finding the coolest, most useful, best designed apps isn't easy. That's why every day I go to Terry's app website, because Terry has a gift for finding exactly those types of apps. Honestly, I don't know how he does it, but he always comes up with these amazing apps that everybody falls in love with (which is precisely why, when it comes to iPhone apps, Terry has built a huge cult following). Check it out at www.bestappsite.com. Also, be sure to check out Chapter 16. It's a bonus chapter that Terry and I created that contains the "20 Apps We Can't Live Without."

Chapter Five

Please
Mr. Postman

Getting (and Sending) Email

 This is an incredibly important chapter, because email is incredibly important. If it weren't for the iPhone's ability to get email, I would have missed an amazing adventure. It all started with a desperate email from a Mr. Mabutuu, who (according to the email) had been a high-ranking government official in the small African nation of Nantango. I soon learned of the overthrow of his small, friendly government through a military coup that nearly cost him his life. He was able to flee to the safety of a small village protected by freedom fighters loyal to his ousted government, but before he fled the capital, he was able to move nearly $16 million of his government's surplus cash (in U.S. funds) to a small bank in a neighboring country. His main concern was that these funds not fall into the hands of the corrupt general who led the rebellion against him, and he asked if I would be so kind as to help him find a suitable U.S. bank where he could wire the $16 million. For my small role in providing my bank account number, username, password, and social security number, he would gladly share the $16 million with me rather than see it seized by the new hostile government (he proposed a 60/40 split, but I was able to negotiate it to 50/50). However, he was in a bind because before his bank would transfer the funds to my bank account, he would have to first pay $22,800 for the required doc stamps and tariffs to complete the wire transfer. Of course, I immediately wired the $22,800 to his overseas account, and since then, each day I patiently check my account for the transfer of the $16 million to hit (that's going to be a pretty exciting day for us both, eh?).

Setting Up Your Email

If your email is already set up on your computer, then you can choose in iTunes which email accounts you want to have working on your iPhone (click on your iPhone in the Devices list on the left of the window, then click on the Info tab in the iPhone's preferences and make your sync choices in the Mail Accounts section). To set up your email directly on your iPhone, tap on **Mail**, then on the Welcome to Mail screen, just tap on the type of email account you have if it's in the list. If your email account is on Apple's iCloud, Microsoft Exchange, Google (Gmail), Yahoo, AOL, or Hotmail, your iPhone will know most of the geeky settings, so all you'll need is your username, email address, and password (if you use iCloud or Microsoft Exchange, see pages 88 and 89). If your account isn't on one of these services, see the next page. By the way, if you have a Yahoo, Gmail, or Hotmail email account, you'll get a free "push" type email. This means that instead of having to check for new messages, the emails will come to your iPhone automatically. Some other types of accounts will need to be checked, which you can set your iPhone to do automatically at regular intervals. The iPhone software also has Microsoft Exchange Active Sync support, but you'll need to check with your company's IT department to get the settings first.

What If Your Email Isn't in the List?

If your email account isn't listed on the Welcome to Mail screen (see the previous page), tap **Other** at the bottom to set it up yourself. You'll need to know at least your username, email address, and password—the iPhone will know the geeky settings for most webmail accounts. If not, you'll need to know:

• your email server type: POP, IMAP, or Exchange
• incoming server address (a.k.a. POP server): mail.domain.com
• outgoing server address (a.k.a. SMTP server): smtp.domain.com

Also, most outgoing mail servers require some kind of password for sending mail when you're not on their network. You'll need to check with your ISP to find out what settings to use. Most ISPs display this info in the help section of their websites. When you set up your account, you probably received an email with all of this info.

---

iTip　Choose IMAP Over POP

If you have a choice between POP- or IMAP-based email, choose IMAP. The reason is that IMAP email resides on a server. When you read an email on your iPhone, it will be marked as read on the server so that when you go to your computer to check email, you won't have to read the ones you've already read. Same goes for trashing an email. Once trashed on the iPhone, it will be trashed on your computer, too.

Add an iCloud Email Account

Apple has their own free service called iCloud, which offers direct push and syncing of your email similar to Microsoft Exchange. (You can also sync your contacts, Safari bookmarks, reminders, notes, music, photos, apps, iBooks, documents/data, and calendar to iCloud and have this information wirelessly sync to your iPhone. For more on iCloud, see Chapter 9.) iCloud includes an email account and when email is received in your iCloud account, if you want to, it can be pushed out to your iPhone instantly. iCloud is a cross-platform service for both Mac and Windows users. Once you have your iCloud account set up, you can set up your iPhone to receive your iCloud email by going to Mail and tapping on **iCloud** (if you haven't set up any other email accounts yet) or by going to Settings, then to Mail, Contacts, Calendars, then tapping on **Add Account**, and tapping on iCloud. Just enter your Apple ID and Password, and you're all set.

Add a Corporate Microsoft Exchange Email Account

You can have direct push of email, calendar appointments, and contacts wirelessly via Microsoft Exchange, without having to sync via the USB cable to your computer. You'll have to first check with your corporate IT department to get the correct settings for your account, and once you have this information, add the Microsoft Exchange account to your iPhone (if you haven't set up any other email accounts yet, go to Mail and tap **Microsoft Exchange**, or from Settings, tap on Mail, Contacts, Calendars, then tap on **Add Account**, tap on Microsoft Exchange on the Add Account screen, and enter your Exchange account information). You'll get the option of whether or not you want your contacts and calendar synced, too, and in iOS 4 and higher, there is support for multiple Exchange accounts. When email is received at your office, it is pushed out to your iPhone immediately. When someone proposes a meeting, you'll be able to respond and have the meeting added to your calendar instantly. Also, any changes to your contacts are automatically synced to the server. So you basically never have to sync this information via the USB cable. Don't throw the cable away just yet, though, you'll still need it to sync your iPhone for music, movies, etc., as well as for iPhone software updates (if you're not syncing all this wirelessly) and to charge it.

Checking Your Email

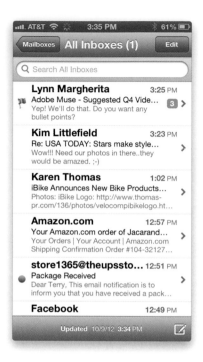

The iPhone is pretty smart in that there really isn't a check email button. It assumes that when you tap the Mail app on the Home screen, you probably want to check your email. Once you're looking at your Inbox, you can also have the iPhone check for new mail immediately on the Mailboxes or Inbox/All Inboxes screen by swiping downward, pulling the whole screen down. The iPhone can check for new email manually, on a schedule (such as every 30 minutes—just go to Settings, tap on Mail, Contacts, Calendars, then tap on **Fetch New Data**, and make your choice in the Fetch section), or if your email account supports it, via "push." For example, Microsoft Exchange and iCloud email is automatically pushed out to your iPhone as soon as it comes in.

---

iTip **Email Download Times and Your Battery**

You can change your settings for Mail to automatically check for new messages every 15 minutes, every 30 minutes, or every hour. The more often the iPhone checks for email, the more it will use the battery. I chose every 30 minutes as a happy medium.

The Unified Inbox

In iOS 4 and higher, you can see email from multiple accounts all in one inbox with the All Inboxes combined inbox. This is one of my favorite features, since I have several email accounts on my iPhone. I can see, read, and respond to email from each of my accounts in one spot. You can get to the All Inboxes combined inbox by tapping on the **Mail app** or by tapping the **back button** from any email account you're currently in.

Getting Email from Your VIP Contacts

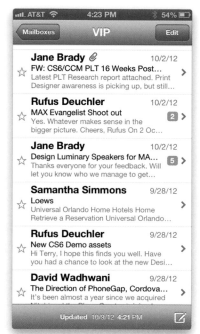

In iOS 6, there's a new way to identify important emails from co-workers, the boss, family, close friends, etc. You can mark a contact as a VIP by tapping on the contact that sent you the email. You'll get their contact Sender screen or the ability to add them as a contact, but on either screen, there's now an **Add to VIP button**. You can also go to the VIP inbox and tap the **Add VIP button**. Once you add a contact as a VIP, any email that you receive from that contact will have a star next to it. Also, if you go to the VIP inbox, you'll see any emails that you've received from any of your VIPs, so you can read and respond to them right then and there. If you no longer want a contact to be a VIP, simply go to their contact Sender screen and tap the Remove from VIP button.

Reading Your Email

Once your email is set up and the messages start rolling in, tap on the Inbox you want to check. Unread messages will have a blue dot to the left of them and the iPhone displays the first two lines of each message. When you want to display the entire email, just tap on the one you want to read. You can scroll through the message by flicking your finger up or down on the screen. If the type is too small, you can use the pinch feature to zoom in and out: using two fingers on the display, such as your index finger and thumb, you spread them out to zoom in on the message, then pinch them in to zoom back out. You can also pan around the message by simply moving your finger around on the display in the direction you want the message to move. You can use the up and down arrows in the upper-right corner to move to the next message or previous message. In a text email, you can double-tap on a word and, from the pop-up menu, choose to Copy, Select All, or Define it.

---

iTip   **Marking a Message as Unread**

*You can mark a message as unread by tapping the Edit button at the top right of the Inbox screen, then tapping on the circle that appears to the left of the message to select it, and tapping the Mark button at the bottom right of the screen. Tap **Mark as Unread** in the pop-up menu and the message will be marked as new.*

Threaded Email Discussions

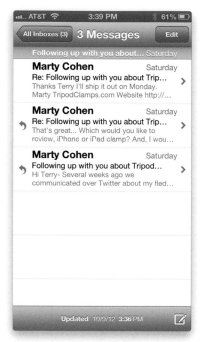

You can view threaded email, and here's how it works: When you receive an email and then you or someone else responds back to it, and then another response from someone is sent, a thread is created. You'll actually see a little indicator with a message count on the right side of the email (when you're looking at it in your Inbox) and when you tap on the most recent message, you'll see all the messages relating to that email thread. This means no more having to scroll down through your Inbox to find the related messages that were sent earlier.

---

iTip   **Is That Email Important?**

*If someone sends an email message directly to you, chances are it's more important than an email that you were only copied on. The iPhone's Mail app lets you see if you are in the To field or in the CC field at a glance—a "To" or "Cc" will be at the beginning of each message that has you in one of these fields. If you don't see this, tap on the Settings app, then tap Mail, Contacts, Calendars, and turn **Show To/Cc Label** on.*

Viewing and Playing Email Attachments

The iPhone supports viewing attachments such as JPGs, PDFs, Microsoft Office documents (Word, Excel, and PowerPoint), and iWork documents (Keynote, Numbers, and Pages). If you receive an image, such as a JPG, Mail shows the image right in the body of the message. If you receive one of the other file types, the attachment will generally be at the bottom of the email message. Simply tap the attachment to view it. The message will slide over to the left and show you the attachment in a separate screen. If you'd rather view the message in a different app that you have installed, you can tap the button that looks like a box with an arrow coming out of it in the upper-right corner to transfer and view that attachment in a compatible app. If you prefer to see the attachment in a horizontal view, just turn your iPhone sideways. Once you're done viewing it, tap the Message button at the top of the screen to go back to the original email. If you have more than one attachment, you can view the next one once you return to the message. You can also play a compatible audio attachment (like an MOV or M4A file) by tapping on it in the email.

iTip **Printing an Email Attachment**

*In iOS 5 or later, you can print your email attachments through AirPrint. With the attachment open on your iPhone, simply tap the button in the top-right corner (the box with the arrow), then tap the **Print button** in the menu that appears. For more on AirPrint, see page 109.*

Saving an Emailed Photo to Your iPhone

If you receive an email on your iPhone with a photo attached, you can add that photo to your iPhone's Camera Roll. Tap once directly on the image and a menu will pop up giving you choices to email the photo to someone else, tweet it, post it to Facebook (if you haven't set up your Twitter or Facebook accounts, it will prompt you to do so), assign it to a contact, save it to your Camera Roll, print it, or copy it to the clipboard, so just tap on **Save to Camera Roll**, and it will be added directly to your Camera Roll. You can see the image you just saved in the Camera Roll by pressing the Home button, then tapping Photos, and then tapping **Camera Roll**. Once you see the image, tap on it to see it full screen and then you can do all the things listed above, as well as set it as a wallpaper picture or send it in a text message by tapping on the image and then tapping on the little box with the arrow at the bottom left of the screen. (*Note:* For more on these options, see Chapter 12).

Opening an Attachment in Another App

iOS does a great job of letting you see different kinds of attachments right in the Mail app, such as photos, Microsoft Office documents, PDFs, etc. However, there may be times when you want to open these attachments in other apps to do more with them. For example, let's say you receive a PDF contract and you need to digitally sign it. Mail has no PDF editing capabilities, but there are several apps that do, not the least of which is the free Adobe Reader app for iOS. Once you have one these apps installed, all you have to do is tap the attachment in your email to open it, and then you should see a button with a box with an arrow coming out of it in the upper-right corner of the screen. When you tap on it, a menu will pop up with a list of the apps that you have that can open this type of attachment (along with Mail, Print, and Copy choices). Once you tap on an app, that app launches and opens the attachment.

Dialing a Phone Number from an Email

If someone sends you an email that has a phone number in it, you can simply tap the phone number to dial it. A box will pop up with the number, along with Call and Cancel buttons. Tap the **Call button**, and your iPhone will automatically switch over to the Phone app and place the call. Once you're finished with your call, you can tap the End button. This will take you back to your email message.

Going to a Website from an Email

The web links in your email message, whether they are text links or links on images, are live. So tapping a link in an email will automatically fire up Safari (the web browser app) and take you to the site that you tapped on in your email. Once you're done browsing the site, press the Home button twice to bring up the multitasking bar at the bottom of the screen, and then tap Mail to return to the message you were viewing. One of the features I really like about the Mail app is the ability to "hover my cursor" over a web address in an email to see where that address really goes. Spammers and phishing scams often use hidden links under what looks like a legitimate address. Bring up the email with the questionable web link in it, and simply tap-and-hold on the link for a few seconds. A menu will pop up showing the actual web address the link will take you to, as well as Open, Add to Reading List, Copy, and Cancel buttons. This also works in Safari with links on webpages.

---

iTip **Bookmarking a Web Link**

Once you're in Safari and looking at the page you went to from the email message, you can bookmark it by tapping the button that looks like a box with a curved arrow coming out of it at the bottom of the screen, and tapping the **Bookmark icon**. *Once you add this Bookmark, it will be automatically synced back to your computer the next time you sync your iPhone (if you have this preference set).*

Filing an Email in a Folder

If you have an IMAP-based email account set up, you can have access to additional folders you set up on your computer to help organize your messages, and you can move your email into any of these folders on your iPhone. Since IMAP account folders reside on a server, the next time you check email on your computer, the mail you moved on your iPhone will be in the folder you moved it to. To move a message to a folder, bring up the message from your Inbox and tap the **Move button** on the bottom toolbar—its icon looks like an arrow pointing down over a folder. You will see a list of folders you can move the message to. Tap the folder you want to move it to and your iPhone will move it. If you have a POP-based email account, you can still use this feature to move a message to the Drafts, Sent, or Trash folders. However, these folders only exist on your iPhone, so the message will not be moved to these folders on your computer.

---

iTip **Adding Punctuation Quickly**

*Here's a tip we learned from our friend, author David Pogue: the secret to quickly adding any punctuation when using the keyboard is to tap-and-hold on the **number/punctuation button**, and in a moment, the number and punctuation characters will appear. Now just slide your finger over to the character you want and then remove your finger. It immediately returns you to the regular alphabetical keyboard. Thanks for sharing that one David—we use it every single day!*

Flagging Important Emails

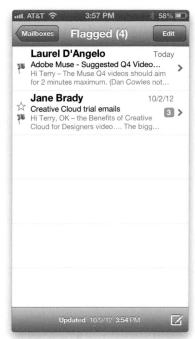

While it's great that iOS lets you file emails in folders, sometimes out of sight equals out of mind. You may forget to go back to an important email or, worse, you may not even remember which folder it's stored in. Mail allows you to flag an email so that you can mark the ones that you want to easily get back to and see again. There's even a Flagged email inbox. To flag an email that you are reading, just tap the **flag icon** in the lower-left corner of the screen. You can also flag multiple emails in your Inbox at the same time by tapping the Edit button while you're viewing your Inbox, then tapping the circle in front of each one that you wish to flag to select them. Tap the Mark button at the bottom of the screen, and then tap the **Flag button** in the pop-up menu. You can remove the flag the same way (the flag button turns to Unflag).

Deleting, Moving, or Marking Emails

To delete messages from your Inbox, tap the Edit button at the top right and a circle will appear next to each message. You can tap the message you want to delete and the circle will turn red with a white checkmark. Once you've selected all the messages you want to delete, just tap the **Delete button** at the bottom left of the screen to delete them. You can move messages the same way: tap on the Edit button, then tap on the message(s) you want to move, and tap the **Move button** at the bottom of the screen. This will bring up a list of folders, and you can tap on the folder you want the message(s) moved into. In iOS 5 or later, you can also flag emails for later follow up, or mark them as read/unread in the same way. From any of your inboxes, just tap the Edit button, select the message(s) that you want to flag or mark, and tap the **Mark button** at the bottom right of the screen. In the menu that appears, just tap Flag or Mark as Read/Unread.

---

iTip Deleting a Single Message Quickly

*While you're reading a message, you can tap the **Trash button** on the bottom toolbar to move the message to the Trash. If you get a message that you know you want to delete without even reading it, you can do it right from the Inbox by flicking your finger across the message. A **Delete button** will appear—tap it, and the message is gone.*

Searching and Handling the Results

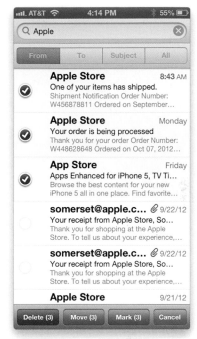

Scroll up to the top of your Inbox, and you'll see a **search bar**. Tap in it, key in what you want to search for, and tap the From, To, or Subject buttons to search in those fields, or tap All to search the entire body of your emails for any keywords or phrases that you want. To get rid of the keyboard, tap the Search button at the bottom right of it. Once your search results appear without the keyboard, you can tap the Edit button in the lower right of the screen, then select each message that you want to move (file away), delete, or mark by tapping on the circle in front of each one. Now, just tap either the **Delete**, **Move**, or **Mark button** to delete the messages, move them to a specific folder, or flag or mark them.

Replying to an Email

Tap the arrow pointing to the left in the toolbar at the bottom of the email (the second button from the right) and you will see a pop-up menu. You can choose Reply, Reply All (if the message was sent to more than one person), Forward, Print, or Cancel. When you tap **Reply**, you'll see a new message already addressed to the original sender and with the original subject. The cursor will already be in the body and all you have to do is start typing your reply. If the original message was sent to you and other people, you can tap the Reply All button to send your reply to the original sender and all the people that the message was sent or copied to. Once you've typed your reply, simply tap the Send button in the upper-right corner. If you tap the Cancel button, you can choose to save or delete the message.

---

iTip **Sending from a Different Account**

*When composing a new message, you'll also see the Cc (carbon copy) and Bcc (blind carbon copy) fields, and if you have multiple email addresses set up, you'll be able to choose which email address you want to send the reply from. Just tap in the Cc/Bcc, From field to activate the Cc and Bcc fields, and then tap in the **From field** to switch between email accounts for sending.*

Forwarding an Email

To forward a message that you're viewing, tap the left-pointing arrow at the bottom of the screen. You will get a pop-up menu where you can choose Reply, Reply All (if the message was sent to multiple people), Forward, Print, or Cancel. Tap **Forward**, and the message appears ready for you to type in the name of the contact, or the email address, that you want to forward it to. If you start typing a name that is already one of your saved contacts, you will see a list of contacts to choose from. The more letters you type, the more it will narrow down the list. If you just want to choose a contact directly, you can tap the + (plus sign) button at the right side of the To field to choose one of your contacts. After putting in your first contact, if you want to forward this message to additional contacts, just start typing in a new name (or email address) and the list will pop up again for you to choose the contact that you want to forward this message to. You can also carbon copy (CC) or blind carbon copy (BCC) additional contacts.

Writing a New Email

To create a new email message, tap on Mail, then tap the **Compose button** at the bottom right of the screen. A blank email will appear with the cursor in the To field. You can then either type in the name of the contact or the email address that you want to send it to. If you start typing a name that is already one of your saved contacts, you'll see a list of contacts to choose from. The more letters you type, the more it will narrow down the list. If you just want to choose a contact directly, you can tap the + (plus sign) button at the right side of the To field to choose one of your contacts. If you want to send this message to additional contacts, just start typing in a new name. You can also carbon copy (CC) or blind carbon copy (BCC) additional contacts. Next, you'll want to type a subject in the Subject field, and then your message in the body field below. Your email can be as long as you like. Once you have your message addressed and composed, you can tap the Send button to send it. If you tap the Cancel button, you'll be given the opportunity to save it as a draft and continue it later.

---

iTip **The Secret .com Button in Mail**

*Did you ever notice that there's a .com button on the Safari app's keyboard, but not in the Mail app? Well, there is one, it's just not obvious. If you want to end an email address with .com, .org, etc., just tap-and-hold on the **period key** until the choices pop up. Then slide your finger over and choose a domain ending. You can actually use this feature with any keyboard with a period key.*

Editing Your Email

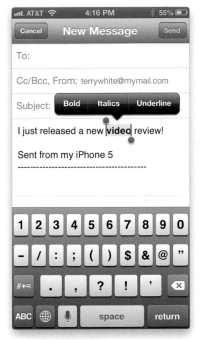

In the same pop-up menu with Cut/Copy/Paste (see page 269), you can add a little format-ting to your email, get word suggestions, get a word definition, or increase/decrease the text indent. For formatting, you can add bold, italics, or underlining to a word or phrase, as well as increase or decrease the indent (Quote Level) of a block of text (when typing a reply). Just tap on Mail, and then tap the Compose button or reply to an existing message. Start typing your email as usual, and when you want to add some formatting, just double-tap the word you want to format. If it's more than one word, you can use the blue handles to extend your selection. At the right end of this pop-up menu is an arrow button. Keep tapping it to show the rest of the choices: Suggest..., BIU, Define, Insert Photo or Video, and Quote Level. Tap on Suggest... to get a word suggestion; tap on BIU, and you'll get a menu with Bold, Italics, and Underline; tap on Define to get a dictionary definition; tap on Insert Photo or Video to bring up the Photos app and choose the photo or video you want to add to your email; or tap on Quote Level to choose Increase or Decrease.

iTip Quote Only Part of an Email in a Reply

If you only want to quote part of the original email in your reply, select the portion you want to quote by double-tapping near the part of the email you want to include in your reply and drag-ging the handles around it. Then, tap the arrow pointing to the left at the bottom of the screen, and then tap the Reply button.

Emailing a Photo

You can email either the photos you take with your iPhone's camera or ones already in your photo Albums. To email a photo, tap Photos. If you want to send one you took with your iPhone's camera, it will be in the Camera Roll folder. If you want to send one you synced from your computer, it will either be in the Photo Library or one of the albums that you brought over. Find the photo you want to send and tap on it. In the lower-left corner is an arrow coming out of a box. Tap that button, then tap the **Mail button**, and it will put your photo into the body of a new message. You can then address the message, give it a subject, type some text in the body area, and tap the Send button. New in iOS 6, you can double-tap right in the body of the message where you want to attach the photo, and a menu will pop up. Tap the arrow at the right end of that menu, then tap **Insert Photo or Video**. This brings up your Photos app, where you can choose any photo (or video) in any album. Once you choose a photo, you'll get a preview of it. Tap the Choose button in the bottom right, and the photo will be inserted in your email.

---

iTip Emailing Multiple Photos

*You can also email multiple photos by going to Photos and selecting the Camera Roll or a particular album. Once the thumbnails are displayed, you can then tap the Edit button in the top-right corner. Next, tap the photos you want to send to select them (you can select up to five), tap the Share button, and then tap the **Mail button**.*

Printing an Email

You can print your email to a wireless AirPrint-compatible printer directly from your iPhone (it must be connected to the same Wi-Fi network as your iPhone). Just bring up the email you want to print and tap the arrow pointing to the left in the toolbar at the bottom. This brings up a menu with Reply, Forward, and Print buttons. Once you tap **Print**, you'll be able to select your AirPrint-compatible wireless printer, choose how many copies to print, and print away.

---

iTip **When Your Printer Isn't AirPrint Compatible**

Sadly, most printers are not AirPrint compatible. However, all is not lost. If you're on a Mac, you can use Printopia to turn your existing printer into an AirPrint-compatible printer. Check it out at: www.ecamm.com/mac/printopia/. If you're on a Windows PC, try AirPrint Activator at: http: //twhite.me/tYinC5.

Sharing a Contact

Tap on the Utilities folder, then tap Contacts, and find the contact that you want to share. At the bottom of their Info screen, tap the button that says **Share Contact**, then choose to share it in an Email or a Message. Once you make your choice, your iPhone will create a vCard (an electronic business card) and attach it to a new message. You can then address the message to the person you want to send the contact to, and once they receive it, they can then import it into their contact manager or iPhone. If you receive a vCard from someone else, you can add that contact to your contacts list, as well.

---

iTip **Seeing Who an Email Is Addressed To**

If you are in an email, and tap on Details in the header, you can see the names or email addresses of the people the original message went to. If you tap one of the addresses (including the sender), and they are not already one of your contacts, you will be able to create a new email to that person, as well as add them to your contacts.

Using Multiple Email Signatures

One of the iOS 6 features that I've been waiting for, for a long time is multiple email signature support. By default, your email signature is "Sent from my iPhone." While you could always change it in the past, you couldn't make different signatures for different email accounts. Now, you can. You can create a separate, unique signature for each of your email accounts. This is great for people that have a personal email account and a work email account on their iPhones. Tap Mail, Contacts, Calendars in the Settings app, and then scroll down to Signature and tap it. You now have a choice of All Accounts or Per Account. If you tap **Per Account**, you can then set up a separate signature for each of your accounts. Once you set them up, you will see them when you compose new emails or respond to emails from those accounts.

Chapter Six
Surfin' Safari
Using Safari, Your iPhone's Web Browser

 Now you gotta admit—the Beach Boys' classic hit "Surfin' Safari" is just about as perfect a title for a chapter on using the Safari web browser as you can get. But as you know, that's where the cohesiveness ends on this page, because the rest of this paragraph really has nothing to do with browsing the web, or safaris, or even the iPhone, for that matter. That's right, this is my "special time" where you and I get to bond on a level that I normally reserve only for close personal friends and men's room attendants. You see, when someone has read as much of this book as you have, a very magical thing happens. It's a magical moment of extreme clarity we both share simultaneously (but not at the same time), and although we experience this together, we do it totally separately, but still as one (which isn't easy to do). For example, it's that moment when you realize that you've already invested so much time in this book that you really can't stop now and you're "in it for the long haul." For me, it's the moment when I realize that you've had the book so long now you can't really return it for a refund. You see, it really is magical. So, put down the book, and take just a moment to close your eyes, breathe deeply, and just let your mind drift off to a place where it doesn't matter that the chapter introduction doesn't actually relate to the content in the coming chapter. That type of thing no longer matters to you because in your mind you're finally free—free to finally reach out and touch that existential neo-ocular nirvana that can only happen in Seattle. I have no idea how to end this gracefully. Hey! Quick—look over there!

Visiting Webpages on Your iPhone

Safari is the iPhone's web browser (its app icon looks like a compass—it's shown circled here). The first time you launch Safari, it will launch to a blank screen with an Address Bar at the top. Tap in the Address Bar to bring up the keyboard and type in the web address that you want to go to. There is a .com button on the keyboard to type in .com for you at the end of a web address (it's a handy time saver). Once you have the address typed in, just tap the blue **Go button**. If you want to type in a different web address, you can clear the address already in the Address Bar by tapping the little X to the right of it. Safari also will launch automatically when you tap on a web address in one of the other apps.

iTip **Finding a Wireless Network**

*Your web and email connections will be faster if you can jump on a wireless network, but finding a free wireless connection when you're on the road isn't easy, unless you know this trick: Go to the **Maps** app and type in "wifi." Then, if you don't have your Location Services turned on, a comma, and the city and state you're in (i.e., wifi, Kennebunkport, ME), and it will pinpoint the location of nearby places with free Wi-Fi. There's also a free app called JiWire Wi-Fi Finder, which can search for not only local free spots, but any open Wi-Fi networks.*

Getting Around a Webpage

Once you get to a webpage, here are some tips for getting around: First, to scroll down the page, you actually use your finger to flick the page up. In most cases, the page will be too small to read, but you can quickly zoom in on a page (that doesn't have a mobile version) by double-tapping on it. This will zoom the display nice and large. To move the page around, just use your finger to drag the page in the direction that you want to go. To zoom out, double-tap the page again. You can also use two fingers in a spreading out motion as if you're expanding the size of the page to zoom in. To zoom out, use your two fingers to pinch the page as if you're making it smaller, because you are.

iTip   **Jumping to the Top of the Page**

If you've scrolled down a long page, tapping on the time at the top of the screen will take you back up to the top of the webpage.

Saving Webpages to Read Later

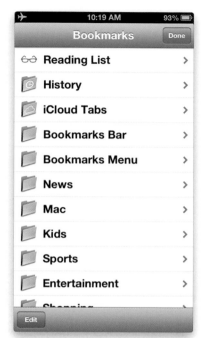

If you see a webpage you'd like to read, but you just don't have the time right this minute, then just tap the center button at the bottom of the Safari browser (the box with the arrow), then tap the **Add to Reading List icon** on the menu that pops up, and it saves that page for later. To see the pages you've saved to your Reading List, just tap on the Bookmarks button (at the bottom of your browser—its icon looks like an open book), and at the top of the list of Bookmarks, you'll see Reading List (with a pair of glasses to the left of it). Tap on that to see the list. *Note:* It just saves the link to these pages. You can't read them offline— you'll need to have Internet access to get to them.

iTip   Open Links in the Background

*When you tap-and-hold on a link in the Safari browser, a pop-up menu lets you open that link on a new page, but if you'd prefer to stay on the same page, and let that new page load in the background (so you can go to it when you're ready, and its fully downloaded), then just go to the Settings app, scroll down, and tap on Safari. Tap on Open Links, and choose **In Background**. That's all there is to it, and now you'll get the choice to Open in Background.*

Getting a New Page and Closing a Page

To get a new page, tap the little Pages button in the lower-right corner of the Safari screen. This will shrink your current page down and a **New Page button** will appear in the lower-left corner. Tap that button to create a new blank page. Now you can either type in a new web address, do a search, or use your Bookmarks to go to the page you want to go to. When you're finished viewing a page, there is no reason to have it out there hanging around, so to close a page that you no longer need open, tap the Pages button, find the page you wish to close, and tap the little red X in the upper-left corner of the page. The page will close and you'll be switched to a page that is still open.

Moving Between Pages

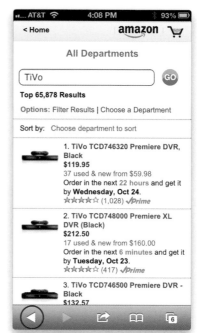

Once you have two or more pages open in Safari, you can move back and forth between them. To go to another open page, tap the **Pages button** in the lower-right corner of the screen. Then, by flicking your finger across the page toward the left or the right, you can move between your open pages. Once you get to the page you want to view, just tap it to bring it back up to full screen. This is really handy when you're trying to compare things, such as prices or schedules, between two different sites at once. Also, Safari has a Back button just like any other web browser, but here it's at the bottom of the screen (it's shown circled on the right here). There's also a Forward button if you want to return to the page you were just on.

iTip See Where That Link Will Take You

If you tap-and-hold your finger down on a text link or graphic link on a webpage, a pop-up menu will appear showing the web address that the link will take you to, and giving you the option to Open, Open in New Page, Add to Reading List, or Copy.

Using Your Bookmarks

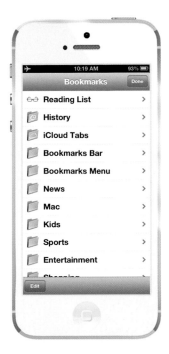

Your iPhone automatically syncs your Bookmarks from Safari on your Mac or PC, or your Favorites in Internet Explorer on your PC (if you have this preference set). To use one of these Bookmarks, tap the little **Bookmarks button** at the bottom of the Safari screen (it looks like a little open book). All of your Bookmarks will be listed just as they appear on your computer. They'll be in the same folders and in the same order. Just go to the Bookmark you want to use and tap it to go to that site.

---

iTip **Refreshing a Webpage**

Safari keeps the page you're currently viewing in place when you switch between apps. However, if you find that you want to know the latest bid on that eBay item you're watching, you may need to refresh the page. You can refresh just about any page in Safari by tapping the circular arrow button at the right of the Address Bar.

Adding a Bookmark

If you have a page open in Safari you'd like to bookmark, tap the center button (it looks like a box with an arrow) at the bottom of the Safari screen and, from the options that appear, tap the **Bookmark icon**. This will ask you to name the Bookmark (you can simply leave it as the name of the page as it appears, or you can rename or shorten the name to your liking). You can also decide where it saves the Bookmark in your Bookmarks folders by tapping on the Bookmarks folder button below the web address. Once you're happy with the name and location of the Bookmark, tap the Save button to save it.

iTip **You Don't Have to Type the Full Address**

It's usually not necessary to type the full address, such as http://www.creativesuitepodcast.com. Usually just typing the domain name and domain extension will work, such as creativesuitepod cast.com.

Editing or Deleting a Bookmark

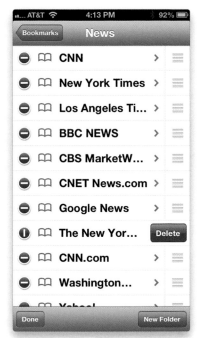

If you want to update or delete a Bookmark, launch Safari and tap the Bookmarks button at the bottom of the screen. This will bring up your Bookmarks list, where you'll be able to find the Bookmark that you want to edit or delete. Next, tap the **Edit button** in the lower-left corner of the Bookmarks screen (or the folder's screen, if it's in one), then tap the Bookmark you wish to edit. You'll be able to edit the name and the web address, as well as its location, then tap the Done button. When you tapped the Edit button, a – (minus sign) in a red circle appeared to the left of each Bookmark. To delete a Bookmark, tap the red circle next to it, and the Delete button will appear. Tap the **Delete button** and that Bookmark will be deleted forever. Once you've made your changes and deletions, tap the Done button, then tap the Bookmarks (or Bookmarks folder) button in the upper-left corner of the screen to return to the Bookmarks list.

---

iTip **Bookmark Changes Will Sync with Your iPhone**

One great thing is that if you update or delete a Bookmark on your computer, it will be updated or deleted in your iPhone the next time you sync (if you have this preference set) or over the air if you use iCloud.

Adding or Removing a Direct Web Link Icon

If there are websites you go to a lot, you can add a web link icon (Apple calls these web clips) directly to one of your Home screens, and you can even have it scroll to the area of the page that you always check out. Just go to Safari, then go to the website you want to add (zoom in on it if you like), and tap the center button (it looks like a box with an arrow) at the bottom of the screen. From the options that pop up, tap on the **Add to Home Screen icon**, and you'll see the screen shown on the left above, where you name your new icon. So, just name it and tap the Add button at the top right, and your new icon will be added to your Home screen. If the website is iOS-aware, your icon will be the site's logo. If not, it'll be a mini version of the page. To remove a web clip, tap-and-hold for a few seconds on it, until all the icons start to wiggle. You'll see a little X in the upper-left corner of each web clip (and app that can be removed). Simply tap the little X and then tap **Delete**. The web clip will disappear, and your remaining icons will reshuffle. Tap the Home button to stop the icons from wiggling and lock them in place.

iTip   Zooming In for Easier Scrolling

If you're on a webpage that is long and requires scrolling, you can of course flick your finger to scroll the page, or you can double-tap to zoom in on the page and then double-tap in the lower half of the page to scroll down a screen at a time (just be sure to tap in a blank area of the page).

Using iCloud Tabs

If you have another device running Safari, such as an iPad or a desktop computer, and you sync with iCloud, you can actually see any tabs you left open on your iPad, computer, etc., right on your iPhone. Not only can you see which sites you were viewing on your other device, but you can tap to view those same sites on your iPhone. Just tap the Bookmarks button at the bottom of your screen and then tap the **iCloud Tabs folder**. You'll see any tabs you had open on your other devices running Safari (6 or later)—just tap the site you want to bring up on your iPhone. This also works in reverse. Any sites you were viewing on your iPhone in Safari will also be available when you get back to your computer or iPad.

Using Google Search

The iPhone is set to Google's search engine by default, and to use it, launch Safari, then tap on the Search field (to the right of the Address Bar) to bring up the keyboard. Now, begin typing in your search terms and as you type, Google will offer suggestions. If you see what you want, just tap on it. If not, just tap the **Search button** in the bottom right when you finish typing. Once your search results come up, you can then tap on any of the links to go to the page that you want to visit. You can also make Yahoo or Bing the default search engine by changing your preference in the Safari settings (tap on the Settings app, then tap Safari, and choose Yahoo or Bing as your **Search Engine**).

Mobile Versions of Your Favorite Sites

Many major websites have a "mobile" version or even a version specifically formatted for the iPhone. This makes getting to the information you want much faster! For example, we've optimized our blogs for mobile devices. If you visit www.terrywhite.com, www .bestappsite.com, or www.scottkelby.com from your iPhone, you'll get the more friendly mobile versions of the websites. Check your favorite site to see if they have a mobile version. Oftentimes, it's as simple as typing "mobile" or "m" in front of the domain name, such as mobile.fandango.com or m.usatoday.com. You may be surprised to see that they even have one that's formatted just for your iPhone.

---

iTip **.org and Other Domains Are One Tap Away**

*Not every site ends in .com, but luckily, you can use the .com button to access the rest of the most commonly used domains on the Internet. If you want to use a different domain ending (such as .org), tap-and-hold on the **.com button** on the Safari keyboard and, once the choices pop up, slide your finger over them and choose the one you want.*

Reading Webpages Made *Much* Easier

 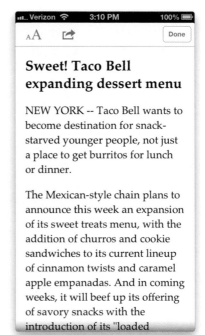

Reading articles on webpages packed with photos, and graphics, and banners, and… well, you get the idea, can be a bit challenging, which is exactly why you'll want to get to know Safari's built-in Reader. When you're starting to read an article, look to the right side of the Address Bar and you'll see a **Reader button**. Tap on it, and it hides all the extra stuff and gives you just the nice, clean, easy-to-read view you see above right. Plus, if you want the type larger, just tap on the "A" button at the top left of the screen to increase the font size (making it even easier to read).

Dialing a Phone Number on a Webpage

If you're looking at a webpage that has a phone number on it, chances are your iPhone will recognize it as a phone number and it will be highlighted or show up as a Call button. You can tap the **phone number** or **Call button** and your iPhone will ask you whether or not you want to dial it. If you tap Call, it calls that number. Once you tap End Call, you'll be returned to the webpage you were looking at last.

---

iTip   Open a Link in Safari to a New Page

If you tap a link on a webpage, Safari will open that link in the same page you were just viewing. But, if you tap-and-hold on a link, you'll get the option to open that link in a new page. This way you can go back and forth between the two webpages.

Filling in an Online Form

When you get to a form on a webpage, you can tap on the first field on that page to zoom in on the field and bring up the keyboard. Type out your response for the first field, and then if the second field is still in view, just tap it and keep typing. If the next field is not in view, tap Done on the keyboard to zoom the page back out again, then you can tap in the field you want to go to next and the keyboard will reappear. You can also use the Previous and Next buttons to move from field to field. If you tap on a pop-up menu on a page, Safari does something very cool: it magnifies the list of choices and puts them in a flick wheel that you can spin with your finger to get to the right option. Once you've got your form all filled out, you can get rid of the keyboard or flick wheel by tapping Done and then tap the submit button for your form to submit your data.

---

iTip **Use the AutoFill Feature**

*When you fill out a form that you'll be filling out on a regular basis, you can use the AutoFill feature to fill out the form with information from the last time you filled it out. To turn on this feature, tap on the Settings app, then tap on Safari, and then tap on **AutoFill**.*

Save or Copy an Image from a Webpage

If you find an image on a webpage that you want to keep, you can save the image directly from the webpage to your iPhone's Camera Roll (where you can then email it, send it in a text message, assign it to a contact, use it as your wallpaper, tweet it, post it to Facebook, or print it), or you can copy it to paste in another app. In the Safari app, just go to the webpage that has the picture on it that you want to save or copy, tap-and-hold on the picture, and a menu will pop up with the options to save or copy the image. Once you make your choice, the menu will go away and the image will be saved in your Camera Roll or copied to your clipboard. Access the image in your Camera Roll by tapping on the **Photos app**, or go to another app (like Mail), double-tap, and then tap the **Paste button** to paste it.

---

iTip **Do Your Browsing in Private**

*If you want to use Safari, but for security or privacy reasons you don't want there to be a history of what you view, just turn on Private Browsing (go to the Settings app, tap on Safari, then tap on the **Private Browsing OFF button** to turn it on).*

Share or Print a Webpage

With iOS 6 or later, you have various ways to share a webpage that you are looking at in Safari. Just tap the center button (the box with the arrow in it) at the bottom of the screen and you'll be able to choose to share a link to the page using Mail, Message, Twitter, or Facebook (provided, of course, you have your Twitter and Facebook accounts set up in the Settings app), or you can print the page if you have an AirPrint-compatible Wi-Fi printer (see page 109 for more on printing).

Chapter Seven
Tool Time
iPhone's Tools for Organizing Your Life

 Are we now to the point that our lives have become so complex, so chaotic, and so congealed (congealed?) that the only way to keep track of it all is to buy a hand-held device which becomes the center around which our lives revolve as it shouts out alarms, and commands us to be in certain places at certain times? All this while we're trying to monitor the markets, and stay in contact with people on different continents, in different time zones, and the only way we feel we can find the location of the nearest coffee shop is to send a request to a satellite in geosynchronous orbit above the earth requesting that it not only point out the location of said coffee shop, but that it ping a different satellite to provide a detailed photographic image of its roof? Is this what we've come to? Yes, yes it is, but I'm totally okay with it. Why? Because I bought stock in numerous GPS satellite companies, Google, and Starbucks. Okay, I really didn't buy stock in those companies but I could have, and I could have done it right from my iPhone. Well, at least until my wife found out, because at that moment you would've heard that cast-iron sound of a frying pan connecting with a husband's head (the one you hear in cartoons), but it would've been so loud that they would've heard it aboard the International Space Station (which is in geosynchronous orbit high above the earth, by the way), and when the astronauts heard it, they'd look at each other, nod, and say, "I bet some guy's wife just found out he bought a whole bunch of stock using his iPhone." You know, it really is a small world after all.

Using Passbook for Gift Cards, Boarding Passes & More, Part 1

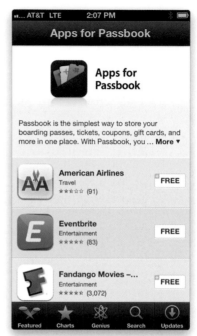

Your iPhone comes with a very cleverly designed app called Passbook that lets you con-solidate all your gift cards, customer loyalty cards, coupons, and even movie tickets and airline boarding passes, all in one handy place. Better yet, Passbook is smart, because your passes appear when you need them (if the retailer supports this), like when you walk into a store or arrive at the airport. It uses your iPhone's Location Services to know where you are and give you the right card, boarding pass, etc., at the right time—right on your Lock screen—without you even having to launch Passbook. To set up Passbook, you'll first need to download the corresponding app from the participating company that you have the gift card, loyalty card, etc., for (for example, if you have a Starbucks gift card, you'll need to download the Starbucks app). So, tap on the Passbook app, then tap on the App Store button at the bottom of the screen. It will take you to the App Store and show you a list of Passbook-compatible apps. (*Note:* Setting up passes from different companies is a little different for each one. But, once you download the participating company's app, you can usually find where to add your card, coupon, etc., under the card, coupon, etc., options. We'll look at how to add a Starbucks gift card pass on the next page. Also, you'll need to be signed into your iCloud account to add passes to Passbook.)

Using Passbook for Gift Cards, Boarding Passes & More Part 2

So, for example, to add a Starbucks gift card to Passbook, you'll first need to download the Starbucks app, if you don't have it already. Once you've downloaded the app, it will prompt you to sign in to your account, and you can then enter the information for your gift card (the numbers on the back of the card). Once it's entered, you'll see a pop-up asking if you want to add the card to Passbook. Tap OK, and the card's "pass" will now appear in Passbook (if you already had a card entered in the app, just tap the Manage button, then tap Add Card to Passbook). The next time you're at Starbucks, they can scan the barcode that appears right within your Starbucks pass in Passbook. If you're emailed a Passbook coupon, you can add that, too: just tap the link in the email and it's added to Passbook automatically (you can scroll down within Passbook to see it). Lastly, there are some extra options for some cards (for example, having your airline boarding pass automatically update you if your gate changes) and to turn those features on, tap on the "i" icon in the bottom-right corner of a pass to see its options (including a trash can button for deleting expired coupons or other passes you no longer need).

Using the Notification Center

iOS 5 and later include a great, somewhat hidden, Notification Center. It's available no matter which Home screen you're on or which app you're in. In the past, if an app gave you a Push notification, a little banner would appear onscreen that you had to acknowledge. Sometimes these notifications would interrupt the app you were in and, worse, if you got a lot of them while you were away from your iPhone, you'd have to go through and acknowledge each one before being able to do anything else. That has all changed. If you get a notification while you're doing something on your iPhone, it will appear briefly at the top of the screen and then go away. If your iPhone is asleep, you'll get an alert on the Lock screen. Swipe the icon in the alert to the right to be taken to that app. If you ever want to see your notifications, just swipe down from the top of your screen to display your current and past notifications. Any apps that are configured to use the Notification Center will list their notifications there. You can clear all the notifications for a particular app by tapping the X, then tapping the Clear button for that category.

---

iTip Change What You See in the Notification Center

*You can choose which apps display notifications in the Notification Center, as well as reorder them in the list, by going to the Settings app and choosing **Notifications**. Tap the Edit button to be able to drag them in order. To turn off the notification or change the style of notification for an app, just tap on it in the list.*

Using Reminders

iOS 5 and later include a dedicated Reminders app, like a built-in to-do list. In the Reminders app, you can create new reminders by tapping the + (plus sign) button in the top-right corner. Then, just type your reminder and tap Done. Simple reminders will appear in your list with an empty checkbox by them. Once you complete the task, just tap the box to add a checkmark to it. If you want reminders that actually remind you to do something, tap on the reminder in the list, then choose a particular day, or even set up a location reminder (location reminders don't work with Microsoft Exchange accounts, and if you have reminders turned on in your Mail settings, you'll need to turn them off). Location reminders are cool because they pop up to remind you when you arrive or leave a location of your choosing. You can also set priorities for your reminders to order them in the list, create multiple lists, and if you have a free iCloud account, your reminders will sync there.

---

iTip   Create New Reminders Lists

*To create a new Reminders list (i.e. Home, Work, Grocery, etc.), on the Reminders screen, tap the button in the top left that looks like three horizontal lines, then tap the Edit button in the top right. Tap **Create New List** and type in a list name. You can change lists by swiping side-to-side.*

Using Newsstand

Although most electronic magazine reading is probably done on the iPad, that doesn't mean that users won't want to read them on the iPhone, too. Luckily, in iOS 5 and later, you can consolidate all your iPhone-compatible publications in one spot called Newsstand. Many of these publications are free, and most that cost include a free first issue, so that you can check it out. The easiest way of finding iPhone-Newsstand-compatible publications is to head to the Newsstand category of the App Store on your iPhone (or in iTunes). There, you will see all of the iPhone-Newsstand-compatible apps in one place. Once you download one of these, it will appear in your Newsstand. If the app supports subscriptions, new issues will appear in the same place, as they are available. One thing you'll note is that Newsstand acts like a folder for these apps. Therefore, Newsstand can't be put into a folder that you create, because technically it already is one.

---

iTip **Use Siri to Create Reminders**

If you have an iPhone 5 or 4S, you can actually use Siri to create reminders for you. Just say something like, "Remind me to call my sister when I get home," and Siri will set up a location-based reminder for you automatically.

Using the Game Center

Gaming on the iPhone/iOS platform is big business. Games are often at the top of the App Store's most popular apps lists. Since games are so popular, often people want to not only play games, but they want to play games with or against their friends. This is where Game Center comes in. Game Center allows you to log in or create an ID and invite friends to be your online gaming buddies. From there, you can see all your Game Center–compatible games, share scores, challenge friends to play multiplayer games, and see your ranking against all that play a particular game. One of the games I play is Fruit Ninja, and it uses Game Center as its way of hosting a multiplayer game with another Fruit Ninja player.

iTip **Spotting Newly Downloaded Apps**

When you download a new app, Apple makes it easy for you to know which one is new because they add a blue "NEW" banner across the top-right corner of the app's icon. That way, if you have a lot of apps, the new ones don't get lost (and possibly overlooked) within all your existing apps.

Setting Up Clocks for Different Time Zones

Tap on the Clock app, then tap on **World Clock** at the bottom-left corner of the screen. By default, the World Clock screen shows the current times in Cupertino, California, and New York. To delete a clock (we'll delete Cupertino's clock here), tap the Edit button in the upper-left corner, and a red circle with a – (minus sign) appears before each city. Tap the red circle for the one you want to delete and a Delete button appears on the right. Tap Delete and it's gone (the clock—not Cupertino itself). To add a new city, tap the + (plus sign) button in the top-right corner to bring up a city search field and keyboard. Type in the city you want to add (in our example here, I typed in Los Angeles. Actually, I just typed in "los" and Los Angeles, U.S.A., appeared in the list). When your city appears in the list, just tap on it and it's added as a clock. To add more cities, just tap the + button again.

---

iTip   Why the Default Time Is Cupertino

Why does one of the default clocks in the World Clock screen show Cupertino, California? It's because that's where Apple's headquarters (also known as "the mothership" to Macintosh fanatics) is located.

Using the Stopwatch

In the Clock app, tap on **Stopwatch** at the bottom of the screen to bring up the Stopwatch screen. There are only two buttons: Start and Reset. To start timing something, tap the green Start button. Once the stopwatch starts running, the green Start button is replaced by a red Stop button. To start over, tap Stop, then tap the Reset button. If you want to record lap times, just tap the Lap button (what used to be the Reset button before the stopwatch started running), and those times are listed in the fields below the two buttons. You can have lots of individual lap times (I stopped at 32 laps—man, was I tired), and you can scroll through the list of lap times just like you would scroll any list—by swiping your finger on the screen in the direction you want to scroll.

---

iTip How to Tell It's Nighttime

When you're looking at the time in the World Clock screen, if the clock's face is white, that means it's daytime in that city. If the clock's face is black, it's night.

Setting Up a Countdown Clock

If you need to count down a particular length of time (let's say you're baking and you need to know when it's been 35 minutes), you can set a countdown timer to alert you after 35 minutes has passed. To do this, in the Clock app, tap on **Timer** at the bottom-right corner of the screen to bring up the Timer screen. You can scroll the Hours and Minutes wheels onscreen to set the amount of time you want to count down to. Just below the countdown wheels is a button called When Timer Ends, where you choose either the ringtone that your iPhone will play when the countdown clock hits zero, or you can choose to have the iPhone simply stop playing and go to sleep (which is great if you want to play music for a specific amount of time before you fall asleep, and then have the iPhone put itself to sleep to save battery life). Once you've set your countdown time, and selected what happens when the timer hits zero, just tap the green Start button and the countdown begins.

---

iTip   Siri Can Count Down for You

Siri, on the iPhone 5 or 4S, knows about the built-in timer. Just ask Siri to "Set a timer for 35 minutes" (or whatever amount of time you want), and Siri will set and start the timer.

Using Your iPhone as an Alarm

In the Clock app, tap on **Alarm** at the bottom of the screen to bring up the Alarm screen. To add an alarm, tap on the + (plus sign) button up in the top-right corner of the screen. This brings up the Add Alarm screen, where you can choose whether, and how often, to repeat this alarm, what sound will play when the alarm goes off, whether to allow you to snooze the alarm, and the name of the custom alarm you just created (that way, you can save multiple custom alarms, which is handy if you have to wake up at different times on different days). When you've set up your alarm the way you want it, tap Save and your alarm appears in your Alarm list, and it's turned on. At the set time, your alarm sounds (and will keep sounding) until you tap on the Snooze button (if you turned that feature on), tap-and-slide the Slide to Stop Alarm button, or press the Sleep/Wake button at the top of your iPhone. If you tap Snooze, the alarm sound stops, but it will re-sound in 10 minutes. If you Slide to Stop Alarm or press the Sleep/Wake button, it turns the alarm off. Also, if you want to turn on an alarm you've already set, you can turn on/off alarms in the Alarm list.

iTip Use Siri to Set an Alarm

If you have an iPhone 5 or 4S, you can actually ask Siri to set an alarm for you. Siri understands commands like, "Wake me at 7:30 a.m." Siri will set the alarm and confirm it with you.

Using the Calculator

When you tap on **Calculator** in the Utilities folder, it will bring up a basic calculator. This calculator does all the basic functions that you would expect, such as add, subtract, multiply, and divide, and it has a built-in memory function, too. If you want a more sophisticated scientific calculator (with sine, cosine, tangent, logarithm, etc.), just turn your iPhone sideways and you'll get the Scientific Calculator instead of the basic one. Pretty neat!

---

iTip **Clearing Calculator Mistakes**

*If you make a mistake while entering a series of numbers, you don't have to start over again. Just tap the **C key** once and that will perform a Clear Entry, and then you can simply re-enter the number. Also, to delete an individual number you typed by mistake, just swipe your finger over the display and the last number you entered will be deleted.*

Using the Built-In Maps App

The Maps app uses your iPhone's built-in GPS feature to let you find anything from the nearest golf course to a dry cleaner, and can give you turn-by-turn directions on how to get there. Tap on the **Maps app** and, when the Maps screen appears, you'll see a search field at the top where you can enter an address you'd like to see on the map. Then, tap the blue Search button in the bottom-right corner and it pinpoints that location on the map. We love the Maps app for finding things like local restaurants, or car washes, or stores. For example, if you wanted to find the nearest Dunkin' Donuts (and I know you do), just type "Dunkin' Donuts" in the search field, tap the Search button, and if there are any near you, they'll show up on the map marked with red pushpins (as seen above) and a little pop-up menu. If you tap the blue arrow button in that pop-up, it takes you to a Location screen for that particular pin. If you tap the phone number, it dials it for you (that way, you can ask them how long before the chocolate frosted ones are ready. Mmmmm-mm...donuts). If you want to find a business that isn't near you, just add the city into the search. For example, typing "Dunkin' Donuts, Boston" would locate the ones in, or close to, Boston. To zoom the map in closer, just double-tap on the screen.

---

iTip **Changing the Map Orientation**

*If you've located yourself in Maps, you can tap the **Show Your Current Location button** once more to change the orientation of the map to the direction that you're facing.*

Locate Yourself on the Map

To have the Maps app show you your current location, just tap the **Show Your Current Location button** in the bottom-left corner of the screen (it's shown circled here in red) and your location will appear on the map as a blue dot with a little circular radar beacon pulsing out from it. Now, you can search the surrounding area for the nearest businesses and services by just typing in either a category (like pizza or pharmacy), or the business name and/or address, tap the Search button, and Maps will drop a red pushpin on the results.

---

iTip Getting Walking or Public Transit Directions

*If you want to walk to the address you entered in the search field, or if you want to take public transit, just tap the **Get Directions button** (to the left of the search field) and, at the top of the screen, you'll see three buttons with icons. Tap the center button with the icon that looks like a person walking for walking directions, or tap the button on the right with the bus icon for public transit info, then tap the blue Route button in the top right.*

Turn-by-Turn Driving Directions

You can use the Maps app to hear turn-by-turn driving directions to or from any location. Say you want directions to your favorite restaurant—for me, it's City Fish Grill. Tap in the search field, then type in the name of the location you want to drive to, and then tap on it in the search results or tap the Search button. Once it drops a pin on the map at that location (if there is more than one pin, tap on the one you want), tap the **little green car button** to the left of the pin's name (Location Services must be turned on in the Privacy settings of the Settings app to use your current location), and your iPhone automatically plots your route. Tap the blue Start button in the top right to begin your turn-by-turn directions. If you prefer a written turn-by-turn list of directions, tap the button with the three lines on it at the bottom left. To cancel a route after it has started, tap the End button in the top-left corner. If you want a different starting location, tap on the blue arrow button to the right of the pin's name, then tap the Directions to Here button, tap in the Start field, and type your starting address.

---

iTip   Let Maps Find the Airport for You

Quick, what's the address of the nearest airport? You don't really have to know, because the Maps app has got you covered. All you need to know is the airport code (or just the name of the airport). For example, if you were trying to get to Newark International Airport, simply tap on the Maps app and type "EWR airport" into the search field. Tap the Search button and the Maps app will zero right in on the airport's location.

Drop a Pin on the Map

There will be times that you may not know the exact name of a business you want to find, or even the address you're trying to get to, but you kinda know approximately where it is. If you can find its general location on the map, you can use the Drop Pin feature to put a pin on the map and once in place, you can use it as a reference point to get directions from where you are to the location that is marked by the pin. Tap on the Maps app, then get to the general vicinity that you want to go to on the map—you can do a search for a city, or a street, or anything else that's in the area (or just tap-and-hold on the map and scroll your way to where you want to be). Then, tap on the curled page in the lower-right corner of the screen to get to the other Maps options. Tap on the **Drop Pin button** to put a purple pin on the map, and then you can move the pin around by just tapping on it and dragging it with your finger. Once the pin is in place, tap the pin, then tap the green car button at the left end of the pop-up, and Maps will plot a route from where you are to where the pin is.

---

iTip Revisiting Recent Searches

*If you want to search for an address or business you searched for recently, just tap the button in the top-right corner of the Maps app (just to the right of the Search field—its icon looks like an open book). Tap on the **Recents button** at the bottom of the screen and a list of recent searches will appear where you can just tap the one you want.*

Seeing a Satellite Photo View of Your Map

You can view the map in the Maps app in a few different ways, including from a photo-graphic satellite view, by tapping on the **curled page** in the lower-right corner of the map screen. Tapping Standard shows you an illustrated map of the location that you search; Satellite will show you an actual satellite photo of the location you search; and Hybrid shows you the Satellite view with the street names—this is kind of the best of both worlds.

---

iTip **Rotating the Map**

You can move around the map by just tapping-and-dragging the map screen, but if you want to rotate the map, put two fingers on the screen and twist in the direction you want to rotate. This brings up a little compass icon in the top-right corner of the map and if you want to return to normal view (with north facing upward), just tap on that icon.

Seeing a 3D Map Flyover (This Is Really Cool!)

The Maps app lets you see any map in 3D, but even cooler, it lets you do a 3D flyover (like you were flying slowly over a city in a helicopter) over a number of major cities (like New York, Copenhagen, Chicago, Montreal, San Francisco, Miami, Los Angeles, and Las Vegas, among others). You start by tapping on the curled page in the lower-right corner of the screen to get to the other Maps options and then tap on Satellite. Next, zoom in on the map location of a major city (pinch-and-spread your fingers on the map screen). If the 3D button changes into a building icon, Flyover is available. So, tap the **Flyover button**, or just press two fingers on the screen and drag upward to enter 3D Flyover view. Now, you can just swipe to fly around the city seeing the buildings in 3D (pretty amazing really, and we can't wait until they add even more cities). One tip: when the 3D photographic maps are drawing, it might take a few moments before they appear, so just be patient for a few seconds and then start flyin'!

---

iTip **Seeing and Hearing Your Directions from the Lock Screen**

If you're using the turn-by-turn navigation feature and your iPhone goes to sleep, you don't have to unlock your phone to get back to the Maps app to find out which turn to make next. The directions will still show on the Lock screen and you'll continue to hear them, as well.

Seeing Real-Time Traffic Conditions on Your Map

If you want to see the traffic for a route you'll be taking, tap on the curled page in the lower-right corner of the screen to see the other Maps options and then tap on the **Show Traffic button**. The traffic is displayed in color-coded dots, so if you see red dots, you know it's stop-and-go traffic (so you're probably in Los Angeles on the 110), or if you see orange dots, then it's just slow traffic (still on the 110, but it's after 9:00 p.m.).

---

iTip **Controlling the Volume of Your Voice Navigation**

To change the volume of the turn-by-turn navigation feature, tap on the Settings app, then scroll down and tap Maps. You can set the volume to low, normal, or loud, or you can choose to have No Voice, which mutes the spoken turn-by-turn directions. While you're there, you can see that you can also choose to view your distances in miles or kilometers, and you can choose how large (or small) to view map labels.

Finding Your Contacts on the Map

You can search for your contacts in the Maps app if you have their street address in your contacts list. Let's say that you want to map a route to one of your contacts and call them before you head out. Well, you can do it all from the Maps app. When you start typing your contact's name in the search field, the Maps app starts searching through your contacts (and the web). Once you find the contact you want, just tap on it and Maps will locate their address on the map. Better yet, tap on the curled page in the lower-right corner of the screen, then tap on the Satellite button, and it shows you a satellite photo of their property. To zoom in for a closer look, just double-tap on their location on the screen. If you want to call them, just tap the blue arrow button to the right of the pin name, and you'll be taken to the contact's Info screen, which has the phone number (if you entered one). You can then just tap the phone number to dial it.

Build Up Your Contacts from the Maps App

If you look up a business by searching in the Maps app, and it's a business that you plan to continue to visit or call, why not have Maps add it to your contacts list? Tap on the Maps app and then search for the business you'd like to add. Once you find it, tap the blue arrow button to the right of the pin name. On the Location screen that appears, scroll down and you'll see an **Add to Contacts button**. Tap it, then tap Create New Contact, and then tap Done, and this information will be added to your contacts list.

Use Map Bookmarks

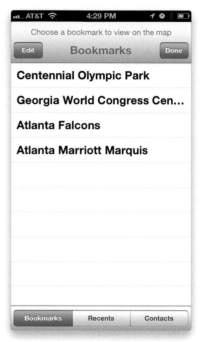

If you're traveling and you want to always be able to get back to the same place or have the same starting point (say your hotel) for each place you want to get a route to (or you get directions to places from home or work a lot), you can save your favorite locations as Bookmarks. You can create a Maps Bookmark from any of your search results or a dropped pin. Just tap the blue arrow button to the right of the pin's name and then tap **Add to Bookmarks**. You'll be able to name the Bookmark whatever you like. Then tap the Save button. Now, the next time you want directions to or from that location, you can use your Bookmark as a start or end destination in the Directions fields. Just tap on the Bookmarks button (the open book icon) at the top right of the screen and, in the Bookmarks screen, choose your location. It will then appear on the map. Tap the Get Directions button in the top left and the location will automatically be entered in the End field. If you want it to be your starting destination, just tap on the curved arrow button to the left of the Destination fields.

---

iTip **Switching Apps and Getting Back to Your Map Fast**

If you're using the turn-by-turn navigation and need to switch to another app, no problem, just press the Home button and choose any other app. You'll see a green banner appear across the top of the screen which reads, "Touch to return to Navigation," which is all you have to do to jump right back to your Maps app and your turn-by-turn nav.

Using the Weather App

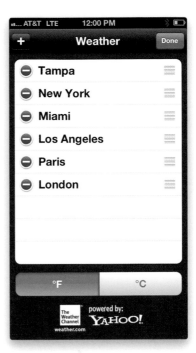

Tap on the **Weather app**, which brings up the local weather based on your location (if Location Services is turned on). You'll also see a detailed 24-hour forecast for that day (swipe to the left across it to see the rest of the day), along with the forecast for the next five days. You can add other cities by tapping once on the little "i" button in the bottom right to bring up the Weather screen. To add your city's weather, tap on the + (plus sign) in the top-left corner, type in your city and state/country or zip code, then tap the Search button. Tap on your city in the results (if it finds it), then tap the blue Done button in the upper right. To delete a city, in the Weather screen, you'll see little red circular buttons in front of each city. Tap on a button and then tap the Delete button that appears to the right to get rid of that city. To reorder the cities, tap-and-hold on the triple-line icon to the right of each city and drag it up or down in the list. To see the weather in different cities, swipe to the side, and the next city slides into place (or tap on the dots below the weather). By the way, on the bottom left of each city's screen is a little Yahoo! logo. Tap on that logo, and it takes you to a Yahoo! webpage with information about that city.

---

iTip   **How to Tell Day and Night in Weather**

The color of the Weather screen lets you know whether it's day or night in the city you're looking at. If the Weather screen appears in blue, it's daytime, and if it's a dark purple, it's night.

Making Quick Notes

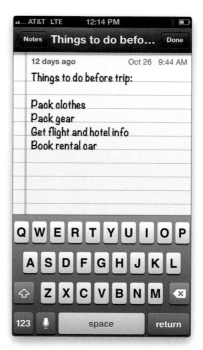

Tap on the Notes app and when the Notes screen appears, you'll see a list of any notes you've already taken. Tap the **+ (plus sign) button** in the upper right to create a new note, or if you haven't created any notes yet, it brings up the New Note screen. Type in your note (using the keyboard at the bottom of the screen), then tap the Done button in the upper-right corner. To return to your list of notes, tap the Notes button in the top-left corner. To read any note in the list, just tap on it (each note automatically displays the date and time it was created at the top of the note). To delete a note, tap on it, then in the next screen tap on the Trash icon at the bottom of the screen. There are little left and right arrow buttons that appear at the bottom of any note, and tapping on one takes you to either the previous note (the left arrow) or the next note in the list (the right arrow). You can enable Notes syncing in iTunes (on the Info pane in your iPhone's preferences), so that Notes sync between your computer and your iPhone. You can also sync them wirelessly through iCloud (see Chapter 9 for more on iCloud).

---

iTip **Editing an Existing Note**

In the Notes app, to quickly edit an existing note, just tap on it in the Notes list. Then when the note appears full screen, just tap anywhere on the note, and the keyboard appears—ready for editing. When you tap, if you tap on a word, your cursor appears right on that word. If you want to add to a note, tap just below your text.

Getting Stock Quotes

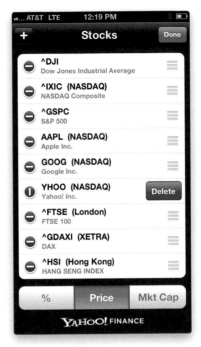

Tap on the Stocks app and when the Stocks screen appears, by default, it shows the Dow Jones Industrial Average and a few other stock indexes, along with a default list of stocks (Apple, Google, Yahoo, and your carrier). You can delete any of these and add your own stocks by first tapping on the little **"i" icon** in the bottom-right corner of the screen. This brings up a list of your current stocks with a red circular – (minus sign) button before each one. Tap on the red – button for the stock you want to remove and a Delete button appears to its right. Tap the Delete button and that stock is removed. To add a new stock, tap the + (plus sign) button in the upper-left corner, type in the company name, index name, or stock symbol (if you know it) on the keyboard, then tap the blue Search button at the bottom-right corner of the screen. When it finds your stock, it will display it in a list. Tap on the name and it's added to your list of stocks. When you're done adding stocks, tap the blue Done button in the upper-right corner. To see all your listings, just scroll down the screen by swiping (or "flicking") your finger from the bottom of the screen up.

Getting More Info on Your Stocks

At the bottom of the Stocks screen, you will see a chart of your currently selected stock's performance over time. To see the stock price information, just swipe (or "flick") to the right on that area (flick a second time, and you'll get news headlines related to that stock). To see a larger chart, turn your iPhone sideways and the graph for your selected stock will take up the whole screen. To change the time frame of the chart, just tap on a time frame at the top of the chart (they range from 1 day to 10 years). For even more information on your currently selected stock, tap on the little Yahoo! logo that appears in the bottom-left corner of the Stocks screen, and it takes you to a Yahoo Finance webpage with detailed information about the company, including recent news articles. To return to your Stocks screen, press the Home button, then tap on the Stocks app, or press the Home button twice to bring up the multitasking bar and tap Stocks.

---

iTip **Changing Stock Price Views**

*To toggle between displaying the stock price's gain or loss in numbers, the gain/loss as a percentage, and its market capitalization, just tap directly on the **numbers** themselves (if the stock is showing a gain, the numbers appear with a green background. If the stock is showing a loss, the background is red).*

Using Stocks as a Currency Converter

The Stocks app has a hidden feature—you can also use it as a currency converter and have current conversion rates at all times. You will need to know the official three-character symbol for the currency you want to track. Tap on the Stocks app and then tap the little **"i" icon** in the lower-right corner. Now tap the + (plus sign) button in the upper-left corner as if you were adding a new stock. Type in the first currency code, followed by the second currency code, and then "=X" with no spaces. For example, if I wanted the conversion from U.S. dollars to Chinese yuan, I would key in USDCNY=X and, as you can see in the example on the left above, it brought up the proper conversion in the search results. Now tap the result you want and tap Done. The main Stocks screen will then show you up-to-date currency conversions whenever you go to it. In my example on the right above, I'm tracking the U.S. dollar against the Chinese yuan, the euro, and the Japanese yen.

Syncing Your Calendar

 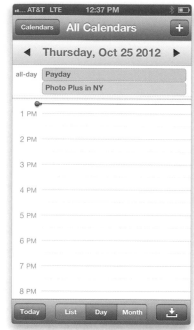

Depending on which calendar program you're using on your computer, you can sync your calendar directly with your iPhone's Calendar app (or you can manually add info to your calendar directly on your iPhone, as you'll learn on the next page). You can sync calendar info from either Apple's iCal or Microsoft Outlook on a Mac, or you can sync your calendar from Microsoft Outlook on a PC. (*Note:* You can also sync your webmail calendars and Facebook events. Just make sure Calendar is turned on in your Mail account and Facebook settings in the Settings app.) You can set iTunes to sync with one of these programs and it will sync your calendar information with your iPhone automatically. If you're a corporate user with a Microsoft Exchange account or an iCloud user, you can sync your calendar over the air, as well. To see your synced calendar info, tap on the **Calendar app**. You can view your calendar as one long scrolling list or in a more traditional calendar view. To view by day, tap the Day button at the bottom of the screen, or tap Month to view the entire month (as shown on the left above). In the Month view, if you see a small dot below the date, that means you have an event scheduled for sometime that day. To see the event, tap once directly on that day and that day's events will appear below the calendar. If you tap the Day view, it shows you the entire day by time, starting at 12:00 a.m. In Day view, you can go to other nearby dates by tapping the left or right arrow buttons near the top of the screen. Any time you want to jump to today's events, just tap the Today button in the bottom-left corner of the screen.

Adding Appointments to Your Calendar

Tap on the Calendar app, then press the **+ (plus sign) button** in the upper-right corner of the Calendar screen to bring up the Add Event screen (as shown above). To give your event a name, tap on the Title field and the keyboard appears so you can type in a title (and a location, if you'd like). Tap on the Starts/Ends/Time Zone field to set the time when your event starts and ends, and the time zone it will be in. This brings up the Start & End screen, where you can choose the start time for your event by using the scroll wheels at the bottom of the screen. Then tap on Ends and choose the ending time. If this event runs the entire day, turn on the All-Day button by tapping on OFF. If you are traveling for the event, choose a time zone, as well. When you're done, tap the blue Done button. When you return to the Add Event screen, there are also options for repeating this event (for example, let's say you have a staff meeting every Monday at 10:00 a.m.—you can tap Repeat, and when the Repeat screen appears, you can choose Every Week, and it will add that event to your calendar every Monday at 10:00 a.m.). If you're using an iCloud, Microsoft Exchange, or CalDAV account, tap on Invitees to invite contacts. If you'd like to get a reminder alarm before your event, tap the Alert button. In the Event Alert screen, tap how long before the event you want the alarm to go off, then tap the Done button at the top of the screen (you can also add a second alarm). If you have multiple calendars, you can choose which calendar you want this event added to. You can also add a website or notes for your event. When everything's just the way you want it, tap the blue Done button in the top-right corner.

Subscribing to Calendars on Your iPhone

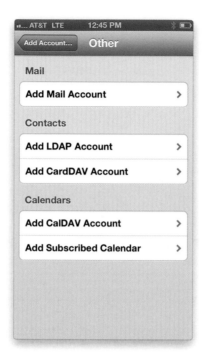

Not only can you sync your calendars to your iPhone, but you can also subscribe to calendars over the Internet right on your iPhone. For example, if your favorite sports team manages a calendar or your spouse publishes his/her iCal to iCloud, you can subscribe to those calendars directly. There are two ways to do this: The easy way would be for someone to email you the link to their calendar (iCal/ICS or CalDAV formats). Once you tap the link in the email, you'll get the option to subscribe to it. If you want to add one manually, you actually don't do it in the Calendar app at all. You go to your Settings app and then go to Mail, Contacts, Calendars. From there, you tap Add Account and then tap **Other**. From this screen, you can choose to add a CalDAV or Subscribed Calendar (ICS format).

---

iTip **Turn on the Birthday Calendar**

*If you add people's birthdays to their contact info (in their Info screen, tap Edit, then tap Add Field, tap **Birthday**, enter their birthday, and tap Done), you can use the built-in Birthdays calendar which appears with the rest of your calendars if it's turned on (tap on the Calendar app, then tap Calendars at the top left, and you'll see it under Other). You can also include your Facebook friends' birthdays in your calendar: tap on the Settings app, then tap on Facebook, and make sure Calendar is turned on.*

Using the Built-In Voice Memos App

You launch the Voice Memos app from the Utilities folder on the Home screen and, when-ever you're ready, you can tap the red **record button**. Once you've made your recording, press the same button to pause the recording or the button on the right to stop it. After you pause or stop the recording, if you press the button on the right, you can go to your list of recordings. From the list, you can play them back, delete them, or share them with others. Depending on your carrier's limits, you may have to trim a longer recording down before you can send it via email or messaging. Luckily, there's a trimming feature right in the Voice Memos app that will appear if the voice memo is too long to send. If it's not too long, but you still want to trim it, just tap the blue arrow button to the right of the voice memo in the list, then tap the Trim Memo button on the Info screen that appears. You can also sync the full length of the recording the next time you sync your iPhone with your computer—iTunes creates a special playlist of voice memos that get transferred from your iPhone.

---

iTip   **Setting Reminders for Birthdays**

*If you have your Birthdays calendar turned on, and you want to get reminders for them ahead of time, just tap on the Settings app, then tap on Mail, Contacts, Calendars. Scroll down to the Calendars section, tap on **Default Alert Times**, and then tap on Birthdays. In the Birthdays screen, simply choose to be reminded that morning, one day before, two days before, or one week before.*

Using the Compass

The iPhone comes with a built-in compass that is not just an app, but a real compass. From your Home screen, tap on the Utilities folder, then tap **Compass** and you'll be able to rotate your iPhone to see which direction you're headed in. If you tap the little "i" in the lower-right corner, you can toggle between Magnetic North and True North. This Compass feature also works in the Maps app to show you the direction you're headed in, if you have Location Services turned on. If you tap the Show Your Current Location button in the bottom-left corner of the Compass screen, it will take you to the Maps app and the map will turn to show you the direction you are facing.

Nike + iPod

The iPhone has a built-in receiver for the Nike + iPod sensor for your running shoes. Since it already has the receiver, all you need to do is purchase the sensor and place it in a compatible pair of Nike shoes. Once the sensor is in place, you can adjust your preferences for Nike + iPod by going to the Settings app. The **Nike + iPod settings** will be in the bottom section, in your third-party application settings area. Once you've got it set, you can then launch the Nike + iPod app from your Home screen and choose your workout and playlist. The next time you sync your iPhone with iTunes, you'll have the option of uploading your results to the NikePlus.com website to track your progress.

Find My iPhone

Before your iPhone is lost or stolen, if you have an iCloud account, you can turn on the **Find My iPhone feature** from within your iCloud account settings on your iPhone. If it is turned on, you can log on to your iCloud account at www.iCloud.com (or in the Find My iPhone app, available for iPhone, iPod touch, or iPad), then click on the Devices button in the top left, choose your phone from the My Devices menu, and then you can locate your iPhone on a map. Now, not only can you locate it, but you can even lock and track it using Lost Mode, as well as play an alert, even if your iPhone's ringer is turned off or it's in Do Not Disturb mode. If you lost it somewhere, you can even display a message that instructs the person who finds it to call you. You can also use this feature to remotely wipe it of all your information and media. Once you initiate a wipe, there is no way to stop it. Even if the person turns the iPhone off, when it's turned back on, the wipe will continue. If you do recover your iPhone, you can simply plug it back into iTunes or use your iCloud backup and restore your data.

---

iTip   Auto-Lock Your iPhone

*Auto-Lock on your iPhone shuts down the display to save battery life and prevents accidental use. The default setting for your iPhone to automatically lock is 1 minute, but you can change this by tapping **Auto-Lock**, in the General settings of the Settings app, and choosing how long you want your iPhone to wait before it automatically locks.*

Secure Your iPhone with a Passcode

No one plans to lose their iPhone or have it stolen. So, if you want a little peace of mind, secure your iPhone with a passcode lock. This will prevent whoever finds it from accessing your data. To set a passcode, tap on the Settings app and then tap on General. Tap on Passcode Lock, then **Turn Passcode On** to turn it on. In the Set Passcode screen, you'll need to enter a four-digit passcode, and on the Passcode Lock screen that appears, you can set an interval for when the iPhone automatically locks by tapping the Require Passcode button. The shorter the time, the more secure the phone will be. You can also choose a more complex passcode with numbers and letters by turning Simple Passcode off. *Note:* Don't worry about having to fumble to enter the code when the phone rings. You only have to enter it when you're making calls or before you go to do other functions. There's also no need to enter the passcode to make an emergency (911) call, to control your Music app, to use Siri, Passbook, or Reply with Message (unless you change those settings).

---

iTip Using Parental Controls

*If you have children that use an iPhone, you can restrict their access to things like installing/deleting apps, buying from the iTunes Store, using content with explicit language, etc. Just tap on Restrictions, in the General settings of the Settings app, then tap the **Enable Restrictions button**. Create a passcode and then set which features you want/don't want your child to use.*

..ıl. AT&T 4G   2:23 PM   * ▭

What can I help you with?

" **What's the best phone** "

Wait... there are other phones?

" **What do you look like** "

Probably not how you expect.

" **What's your favorite**
   color "

My favorite color is... well, it's
sort of greenish, but with more
dimensions.

Chapter Eight
Let's Get Siri-us
How to Use Siri: Your Built-In Personal Assistant

Everybody wants a personal assistant, right? It's so "L.A.-sheik." I know, it's actually "L.A.-chic," but when I wrote that, it looked like "chick," which made me think of the Chick-fil-A restaurant chain and their surprisingly yummy chicken sandwich. They say it has something to do with the fact that they only put one small dill pickle chip on the sandwich, which is kind of odd, because the size of the pickle is disproportionately small when compared to the size of the giant chicken patty. (Of course, I'm not exactly sure it's actually called a "Chicken Patty"—they probably have a more formal name for it, probably something like "Chicken Patricia.") But, unless you really control your bite radius, you're probably only going to get pickle in around 32% of your bites anyway (which is a pretty low ratio, if you ask me), and that means that 68% of the sandwich won't have any pickle flavor at all, which means that most of the time you're eating it you won't even be experiencing the one thing that supposedly makes the sandwich so good in the first place—which is that microscopic lone pickle. If stuff like this keeps you up at night (it does me), then perhaps you should ask Siri, your iPhone's personal assistant, which responds to your voice commands, if she would call your nearest Chick-fil-A and ask them to explain how one tiny pickle can activate an entire chicken sandwich. Because I gotta tell ya—something just doesn't make sense here. And it's not this chapter intro, because of all the things that just don't add up in this world (like how we saw multiple shadows in those NASA moon landing shots, even though there was only one light source [the sun], or how *The Ropers* was cancelled after just one season), I think the fact that our government is clearly not dedicating sufficient resources to addressing this "Pickle-gate" scandal is a national disgrace and the politicians that let this happen should be fired! Of course, when I just wrote "fired," it kind of looked to me like "fries."

Turning Siri On

Siri is even better in iOS 6. It's your voice-activated personal digital assistant, and it's amazing in the way it works. The first thing you'll need to do, though, is turn Siri on (in some cases, Siri is turned off by default). So, go into the Settings app, tap on General, and then tap on Siri. If Siri is off, tap on OFF at the top to turn Siri on. While you're here, you'll definitely want to choose your contact info by tapping on My Info and then choosing yourself from your All Contacts list. This is how Siri will know who you are and your relationships. If you don't have a contact set up for yourself (most people don't), just head over to the Contacts app and create one. Then come back here and assign it to Siri. The more info you put into the contacts you create, such as phone numbers, addresses, and especially relationships (like mother, father, spouse, child, sister, brother, etc.), the more you'll be able to say things to Siri like, "Call my sister."

How to Bring Siri Up

You can bring Siri up one of two ways: The first and most common way is to simply press-and-hold the Home button (she'll come up even when your iPhone is locked or asleep). The second way (if you have it turned on in the Siri settings) is to simply hold your iPhone 5 or 4S up to your ear. Since you're not actually on a call, Siri will assume you want to speak to her, so you can just ask Siri what you want to know. If Siri knows the answer, she'll tell you right off the bat. If not, she may offer to look it up on the web for you. Don't be shy and use plain-English (or your native language, where Siri is available) sentences like, "Wake me at 8:00 a.m." Siri will figure out what that means and set an alarm for you. She'll confirm it with you both verbally and visually. If Siri doesn't understand what you said, she will tell you. Simply tap on the microphone icon and repeat what you said (it may help to speak louder or slower).

What New Things Can You Ask Siri in iOS 6?

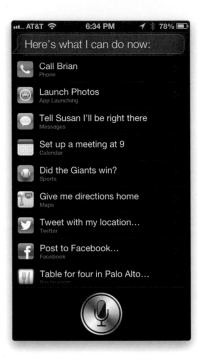

Siri was revolutionary on the iPhone 4S and now, with the release of the iPhone 5 and iOS 6, Siri can do even more! However, at first glance you may not know what new things you can ask Siri. Luckily, Siri can show you what things you can ask. Simply ask Siri, "What's new?" and she will present you with a list of new things that you can ask her.

15 Useful Things to Ask Siri

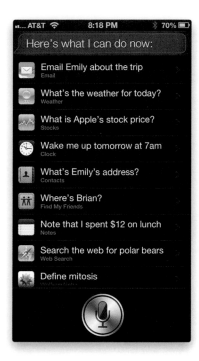

Siri can do and answer lots of useful things that you probably wouldn't think to ask. So, here are a few things to try right off the bat:

- "Wake me at 7:30 a.m." (You can, of course, use whatever time you want.)
- "Call Terry." (Provided that you have a contact named Terry— you get the idea.)
- "Remind me to call Mom."
- "Navigate to my house."
- "What time is it in London, England?"
- "What's 36 times 48?"
- "Play some Janet Jackson."
- "Set up a meeting at 10:00 a.m."
- "Tell Scott I'll call him later."
- "Who won the Tigers game?"
- "I'm hungry."
- "Set a timer for 20 minutes."
- "Post to Facebook…" or "Tweet…"
- "What movies are playing?"
- "What does my calendar look like today?"

15 Fun Things to Ask Siri

While Siri is great at assisting you with day-to-day activities, she also has a sense of humor. So if you ask Siri a silly question, be prepared for a silly answer to come back. For some of these, there are multiple responses, so try it more than once to see what she says the next time. Here are a few to try:

- "What's the best phone?"
- "Beam me up."
- "Knock, knock."
- "How much wood can a woodchuck chuck?"
- "Tell me a joke."
- "Will you marry me?"
- "Where can I hide a body?"
- "What do you look like?"
- "What is your favorite color?"
- "Why did Apple make you?"
- "Hal, open the pod bay doors."
- "Who's your daddy?"
- "Call me an ambulance."
- "Are you conscious?"
- "Are you real?"

Using Siri Over Bluetooth or with Your Headset

Siri's responses to you don't have to be heard by others. If you use a Bluetooth headset or the supplied Apple wired headset, you can use Siri more privately. If you're using a compatible Bluetooth headset, just press-and-hold the talk/answer button on it for a few moments until you hear the Siri beep, or it may say "voice dialing." Then you can speak your command to Siri and hear it back in your earpiece. With the Apple EarPods, just pinch the center of the headset button for a few moments and Siri should activate. If your car has Bluetooth and you've paired your iPhone 5 or 4S with it, Siri may work there, too. In my car, if I hold down the Home button on my iPhone, my car stereo will pause and my voice commands and responses will be played through the car's speakers. It doesn't work with all car Bluetooth systems, but give it a try.

Tips for Better Results with Siri

Siri does a great job out of the box. However, you can get even better results if you ask her things in a better way. Sometimes it's easy for Siri to get confused by the way you ask the question. For example, if you say, "Tell my sister Willie Blue is coming for dinner," Siri will probably respond, "Okay, do you want me to remember Willie Blue is your sister?" Instead, ask Siri to "Tell my sister *that* Willie Blue is coming for dinner." Also, when you have names of relatives that may be hard for Siri to understand, it might be easier to add the relative as a "relationship" in your contact info. That way, instead of asking Siri to call a specific name, you can simply say, "Call my father."

A few more cool things to ask Siri:

- "What is the tip on $25.51?"
- "How much is $15.21 plus Michigan sales tax?"
- "Yahoo, Detroit Lions score!" (Great for games in-progress or the last game played.)
- "Remind me to call home when I leave here." (This will set up a location-based reminder.)

Add to Your Grocery List with Siri

While there are some great grocery list apps for iOS 6 in the App Store, as of the writing of this book, there aren't any that are voice-activated yet. Therefore, you might appreciate this tip on getting Siri to add to your grocery list for you. The first thing you'll need to do is go to the Reminders app and create a new List called "Grocery" (tap on the Lists button near the top left, then tap the Edit button in the top right, tap Create New List to create your new list, then tap the Done button). Now that you have a Reminder list called "Grocery," you can add to this list anytime you want by bringing Siri up and saying something like, "Add bread to the Grocery list," and Siri will create this reminder for you and ask you to confirm it.

Chapter Nine
McCloud
Keep Everything in Sync Using iCloud

 If you just read that chapter title, "McCloud," and thought that was a reference to something on the menu at McDonald's, then you clearly weren't around back in 1970 when NBC aired a groundbreaking TV series about Marshal Sam McCloud (played by actor Dennis Weaver), who was a lawman from out west on temporary assignment with the New York City Police Department, who were kept pretty darn busy back then, because in 1970 they had no simple, reliable way to keep their music, movies, and calendars on their iPhones, iPod touches, and iPads all in sync. I remember this one episode where McCloud (on the show, they usually just called him "McCloud," rather than by his rap name, "Sa-dizzle") was busting these two thugs at West 44th and Broadway, when one of the guys reaches in his jacket pocket to pull out what McCloud thinks must be a gun. So, he dives behind a Ford Pinto Wagon to take cover, but the guy actually pulls out his iPhone instead. Well, of course, McCloud is relieved but takes the iPhone from the thug and starts looking at his Calendar app to see if this guy has any appointments for illegal drug pickups or selling black market 8-track tapes or any of that New York street thug stuff. But, then it hits him—McCloud realizes that the guy just hasn't synced his phone in a while. So, he goes to Crazy Eddie's to buy a sync cable, but the clerk at the counter (played by Buddy Hackett) can't find one anywhere (it's a hilarious scene). So, McCloud has to let the punk go, but as he's handing the thug back his iPhone, a 1971 Datsun B210 careens around the corner, and its side mirror knocks the iPhone out of his hand, and it lands in the street and is crushed by a Ford Galaxie 500 trailing right behind him. McCloud realizes that now we'll never know if the guy was guilty, so he just shoots him. Man, now that was a show!

iCloud Settings

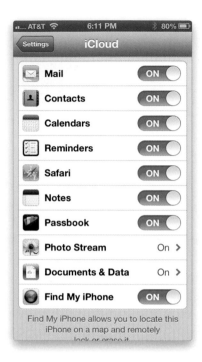

iCloud allows you to sync your Mail, Contacts, Calendars, Reminders, Bookmarks, Notes, Passbook passes, Photos, and documents, as well as back up your iPhone's data. iCloud is free, and once you set up your Apple ID on iCloud, you can go to your iPhone's Settings app and tap **iCloud**. You can choose which kinds of data you want synced (or not) by turning them on (or off) individually. In the past, your iPhone was backed up to your computer each time you plugged it in and synced (if you had that preference set). Now you have the option of turning on the iCloud backup—your iPhone will back up to iCloud each time you plug it in to a power source and you're on Wi-Fi. The advantage is that you can do a restore from anywhere that you have Wi-Fi, in case you have a problem or emergency. Under Storage & Backup, on the iCloud screen, you can also see your available storage (you get 5 GB) or purchase more storage.

---

iTip   Restore from an iCloud Backup

*If something happens to your iPhone and you need to restore it (or a new one) from your iCloud backup, in the Setup Assistant, tap **Restore from iCloud Backup**. Enter your Apple ID and Password, and choose which of the three most recent backups you want to use. Your iPhone will restart, your accounts and data will be restored, and your iTunes Store purchases will start downloading.*

Your Data in the iCloud

The most common use for iCloud syncing is data, like Mail, Contacts, Calendar, Reminders, Bookmarks, and Notes. The advantage of using iCloud to sync this data is that you can update it on your computer or your iPhone and it will update in the other place over the air. You can also edit or view your data at www.iCloud.com. If you're on a Mac running Mac OS X 10.7 Lion or greater, the built-in applications like Address Book, iCal, Safari, and Mail support iCloud syncing. It works well and it's very seamless. If you're on a Windows PC, you can use Outlook 2007 or 2010 and an up-to-date version of your web browser. Apple makes an iCloud Control Panel for Windows Vista and later. You can download it at: www.apple.com/icloud/setup/pc.html.

Your Music in the iCloud

There are two ways to enjoy your music via iCloud. Just by having iCloud and an Apple ID, you can always access your purchased music (or books, or TV shows) from the iTunes Store. Apple allows you to re-download any of your purchases. However, if you go with an iTunes Match account, you not only get access to your iTunes Store Purchased music, but also to all of your music that's been synced to iCloud from your Mac or PC. Yes, even songs that you didn't buy from iTunes. You sign up for iTunes Match in iTunes, and once the process is complete, you can turn it on, on your iPhone. This will wipe any existing music from your iPhone and give you access to all of your playlists and songs. The cost of iTunes Match is $24.99 per year.

Your Photos in the iCloud

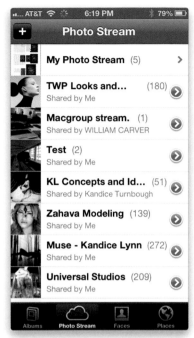

iCloud includes the ability to sync your 1,000 most recent photos between your iPhone, computer, and the iCloud website. Once you turn it on, any photos you take with your iPhone camera will automatically be uploaded to iCloud. If your Mac is running iPhoto 9.2 or higher or Aperture 3.2 or higher, you have Apple TV, or have a Windows PC (with the iCloud Control Panel installed) Pictures Library, and you add photos to any of these sources, they'll appear in the Photo Stream area of your iPhone, too. You can't pick and choose which photos to sync with it, though. It will sync your 1,000 most recent photos, or any photo less than 30 days old. But, you can delete a photo from your Photo Stream. In iOS 6 or later, you can create Shared Photo Streams that you can share with others. With Shared Photo Streams, you can pick and choose which photos to share with each one and these streams can be shared with one or more individuals (they'll also need to have iOS 6 or later or OS X Mountain Lion). People that have access to your Shared Photo Streams can comment on the photos and download them to their devices, too.

Your Documents in the iCloud

iCloud lets you sync documents, too. This means that if you're using Apple's iWork apps (Pages, Numbers, or Keynote), then you can have those documents sync with iCloud. This also means that if you create a Pages document on your iPhone, you could continue editing it on your iPad. You can also sync documents created in iWork '09 or later directly with iCloud on a Mac running OS X 10.8 Mountain Lion or later.

Backing Up to iCloud

You have a choice of being able to back up your iPhone via iTunes on your Mac or PC, or via iCloud. You can turn on an iCloud backup in the Settings app (tap on iCloud, then scroll down and tap on **Storage & Backup**), and when your iPhone is plugged into a power source, is on Wi-Fi, and is locked, it will back up wirelessly to iCloud. You may be wondering what the advantage is of doing it via iCloud vs. your computer, and there really aren't a ton of advantages. One is that it will mean taking up less space on your computer's hard drive. The other, and probably more serious, advantage is that by backing up to iCloud, if your iPhone is ever lost or stolen while you're on the road, you'll be able to replace it with a new one and restore wirelessly from iCloud without having to have your computer with you.

iTip Initiate a Manual Backup to iCloud

*Although your iPhone will back up automatically to iCloud when you plug it into a power source, and it's locked and on Wi-Fi (if you have the backup turned on), you can initiate a manual backup whenever you want just by going to the bottom of the iCloud settings, tapping Storage & Backup, and then tapping the **Back Up Now button**.*

7 of 24

2:18

-1:45

Chapter Ten

I Got the Music in Me

Using Your iPhone's Built-In iPod That's Not Called an iPod

 "Ain't got no trouble in my life. No foolish dream to make me cry." These are the opening lines to KiKi Dee's hit song "I Got the Music in Me," and before we get on to the business of not really talking about the iPod in your iPhone, let's break this down for a moment, because those two opening lines beg more questions than they answer. First, if you're wondering "Who is Kiki Dee?" then we can establish that you do know who Bruno Mars is, which means Kiki Dee is officially old enough to be your mother. *Update:* I just checked and she's now 65 years old, so she could actually be your grandmother, but if your mom was pretty frisky at a young age and had you when she was just out of school, then Kiki Dee could actually be your great grandmother, and if that's the case, you need to give her a call and have a little talk about: (a) Her grammar, which frankly is appalling. "Ain't got no..."? Really? *"Ain't got no"*? Wasn't grammar like a big deal back in the days when she was churning butter with a hand-turned paddle? Anyway, while you've got her on the phone, also ask her (b) why your mom (her granddaughter) was so promiscuous at such an early age, and (c) where she got the name Kiki Dee when her given name was Pauline Matthews [true] or Stella Ludmakker (I made that one up, but if she had been named Stella Ludmakker, she wouldn't have needed a stage name). Anyway, as you can see, this whole Kiki Dee thing opens up a can of worms that I fear could derail the whole purpose of this chapter intro, which is to prepare you to learn how to use your iPhone's built-in iPod that Apple doesn't call an iPod, because they separated the music and video parts into two separate apps, much like your great grandmother once separated the cream from rich whole milk to make what you kids today call "butter," which, not coincidentally, would make a great name for an app about breakfast or *French Cooking with Mademoiselle Kiki Dee*.

If You Have Songs on Your Computer...

…and you want them on your iPhone, you can use Apple's iTunes to sync your songs with your iPhone's Music app. Just connect your iPhone to your computer using the USB cable that came with it, and once you set some preferences, it will transfer your music, playlists, movies, and so on, right over to your iPhone (this can also be done wirelessly, as you'll learn on the next page). However, you probably want some control over how this is done, because your computer has a lot more storage space than your iPhone, and if you have thousands of songs, and hundreds of movies and TV shows, they may not all fit. Luckily, you can choose exactly which songs, playlists, movies, TV shows, podcasts, etc., actually do get transferred over to your iPhone using the little tabs that appear across the top of the main iTunes window when you click on your iPhone in the Devices list on the left side of the window. Take a look at the Music preferences above. When you turn on the Sync Music checkbox, by default, it wants to move all your music over to your iPhone, but if you click the Selected Playlists, Artists, Albums, and Genres radio button, you can choose which of these are copied over (only the ones you turn on a checkbox for will get copied over). You can do this for podcasts, movies, TV shows—you name it. Once you make your choices, click the **Apply button** in the lower-right corner. If you have music and videos on more than one computer, such as a laptop and desktop, then you'll want to manually drag them onto your iPhone instead of syncing them. To do this, connect your iPhone to your computer and click on it in the Devices list on the left side of iTunes. On the Summary tab, turn on the checkbox for **Manually Manage Music and Videos**.

Don't Plug In—Now You Can Sync Wirelessly

In the past, when it was time to sync the music on your computer with the music on your iPhone, there was really only one way to do it—get out the white sync/charging USB cable that came with your iPhone, connect your iPhone to your computer, and then let iTunes sync them. Well, now, at long last, we have the dream—wireless syncing. All you have to do is turn it on (you do have to do one last "connect your iPhone to your computer" to set this up, but once you do, it sets you free from there on out). So, start by connecting your iPhone to your computer using that white sync USB cable. Launch iTunes, and click on your iPhone in the Devices list on the left side of the window, then click on the Summary tab in the main window (if it's not already showing). Near the bottom, turn on the **Sync with this iPhone over Wi-Fi checkbox** and then click the Apply button on the bottom right. Okay, that's it for the computer side of things. Now you have to turn it on, on your iPhone. So, tap on the Settings app, then tap on General, and then tap on **iTunes Wi-Fi Sync**. Make sure the computer you just turned on wireless syncing for is showing below the Sync Now button, then tap the **Sync Now button** and you have just joined the space age, wireless, "developed by NASA for the Space Shuttle Program (not really)" world of wireless syncing. Cut the cord, baby! (Of course, don't really cut the cord—you still need it to charge your iPhone.)

Playing Music on Your iPhone

Once you have music imported into your iPhone, you play it with the **Music app** (I know, it seems kinda obvious). At the bottom of the Music app's screen, tap the Playlists, Artists, Songs, or Albums button to find the first song that you want to hear. Once you find the song, just tap it to begin playing it. If you don't have your headset plugged in, you'll actually hear the music through your iPhone's built-in speaker. If the song has album art, you'll see that while the song plays (if there is no album art, then it just displays a default music note). The song's title, album, and artist appear at the top of the screen. Once your song finishes, it plays the next song in the list. To conserve battery life, after a little while your iPhone's display will go to sleep, but don't worry, the song will keep playing. To get back to the Music app, just press the Home button and unlock the iPhone by swiping your finger across to the right on the Slide to Unlock button. *Note:* Although you launch the Music app to choose which playlist or songs you want to listen to, once you actually start a song or audiobook playing, you can then switch over to and start using other apps, or play games, or whatever, and your music (or audiobook) keeps playing. This works for audio podcasts, as well, and in other audio apps (like Podcasts or Pandora).

Seeing Your List of Songs

When you launch the Music app, at the bottom of the screen you will have buttons that will take you directly to your playlists, or a listing of artists, songs, or albums. There's also a More button to take you to other categories like Compilations, Composers, and Genres. To find a song, just tap the **Songs button** at the bottom of the screen and you'll get an alphabetical list of all the songs in your iPhone's Music app (the songs are listed by title, but the album and artist are listed below each song). If you want to jump to a particular letter in the alphabet, just tap on that letter in the list of letters running down the right side of the screen, and it jumps to songs that begin with that letter. (*Note:* You can also just slide your finger up/down this list and the song list will scroll up/down the alphabet right along with you.) When you find a song you want to hear, just tap on it, and that song's screen appears, and it starts playing.

---

iTip **Seeing Your Song Count**

*If you want to see how many songs you have on your iPhone, tap the **Songs button** and scroll down to the bottom of the list. You can see your song count listed there.*

Searching for Songs

If you've got hundreds, or even thousands, of songs in your iPhone's Music app, you're gonna love the built-in search feature (you just have to know where to find it, because it's not that obvious at first). For example, if you want to search for a song in the Music app, flick downward on any category screen. A **Search field** appears at the top of the screen. Tap in the field, and the keyboard will appear. Just start typing in the name of the song, or artist, you want to listen to, and as soon as you start typing just a few letters, the results appear onscreen. There is the system-wide Spotlight search feature (which you get to by flicking to the right from your first Home screen) that searches everything on your iPhone, but by going to the Music app first, it just searches your Music app, so it's easier to get right to the song you want.

Buying Songs on Your iPhone

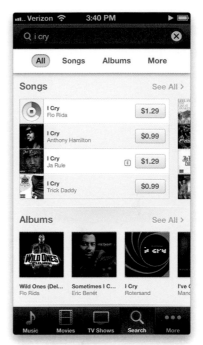

Apple's iTunes Store is the biggest music store in the world, with millions of songs to choose from, and buying songs there is simple. Launch the iTunes app, and its homepage shows you the latest releases. There are top-10 lists when you tap the Charts button at the top, or you can browse by genre (tap the Genres button), but if you know the song you're trying to find, just tap the Search button (at the bottom right), and type in the name of the song you're looking for, or the band or album name. When your search results appear, you can listen to a 90-second preview of the song (to make sure it's the version you want) by tapping once on the album art. If you want to buy that song, tap the price button (at the time this book was published, songs in the iTunes Store cost 69¢, 99¢, or $1.29 US), then tap the **Buy Song button**. It'll ask you for your Apple ID (to make sure it's you), and then the song downloads. It's normally a quick download, since it's a small audio file. To hear the song you just bought, go to your Music app, tap on Playlists, then tap on Purchased, and the last song at the bottom of the list is the one you just bought. To hear it, just tap on it.

---

iTip See a History of Which Songs You've Previewed

If you want to see a running list of which songs you've listened to a preview of, when you're in the iTunes app, tap on Music, then tap on the button in the upper right with the three horizontal lines. That'll bring up a page with your preview history, showing the song info and when you previewed them. Handy for finding a song you liked a while back, but didn't, or couldn't, buy then.

Buy the Rest of an Album (or TV Show Season)

If you have a few songs from an album and want to buy the rest, you can do that right on your iPhone. Start by tapping on the Artists or Albums button at the bottom of the Music app (it has to be one of those two buttons, otherwise the option won't appear), then tap on an artist or album, and it lists the songs you have from that artist (or album). If there are other songs from the album that song appears on, after a few moments a button will appear that says "**Show Complete Album**" (as seen above left). Tap that button and a list appears of all the songs in that album that you don't already have, and you can buy them individually right there on the spot (it doesn't let you play previews of the songs, though. You'd have to go to the iTunes app or iTunes on your computer for that), or scroll down to the bottom and there's usually an option to buy them all. Same thing for TV show seasons— if you're missing a few episodes, now you can download those, too!

Play/Pause, Skipping Songs, Rewind & Volume

To play any song, just tap on it and it starts playing. To pause the song, tap the Pause button (it looks like two vertical lines), which appears at the bottom center of the screen when you're playing a song. Once you've paused a song, that Pause button turns into a Play button (it looks like a right-facing triangle). You can jump to the next song by tapping the right-facing double arrows next to the Play/Pause button. To jump back to the beginning of the current song, tap the left-facing double arrows once, and to jump back to the previous song, tap the left-facing double arrows twice. If you want to fast-forward through a song, tap-and-hold the right-facing double arrows. To rewind, tap-and-hold the left-facing double arrows. If you're wearing the EarPods (headset) that came with your iPhone, there is a little microphone right on the cable, but it's also a button—to pause the current song, press it once; to jump to the next song, press it twice quickly. If your iPhone is locked and you want to pause the music for a moment, just press the Home button twice, then tap the Pause button that appears near the top of the screen. As for volume, there are two ways to adjust it: Use the onscreen volume slider that is at the bottom of the Music app screen—just tap-and-drag the knob (circle) to the right to make the volume louder, or to the left to lower it. The other way is to use the physical volume buttons on the left side of your iPhone. These are the same buttons that you use to adjust the ringer volume and call volume, too. So, those are the basics for playing, pausing, fast-forwarding, rewinding, and controlling your volume.

Your Options When Playing a Song

When you're playing a song, some controls appear at the very top of the screen. To return to the previous screen, tap the Back button at the top left (for example, if you were listening to a playlist, it takes you back to the Playlists screen). If you tap the button at the top right, it takes you to a list of songs from that album (if you have more than one song from that album, you'll see them all listed there. If this is the only song you have from this album, it'll only list this one song). This is also where you can rate the current song (using a 1- to 5-star rating system. See page 206 for more on ratings). Also near the top of the music playing screen is a set of controls with four different options: (1) tap the icon on the bottom left to repeat the song or playlist, (2) use the slider in the top center to "scrub" (move) through the song, (3) tap the icon on the bottom right to shuffle the songs in that album or playlist, and (4) tap the atom icon at the bottom center to have the Music app create a Genius playlist of similar songs based on the song that's playing (see page 205 for more on Genius playlists).

---

iTip   **Control Your Music from Your Lock Screen**

If your iPhone is locked, you can still control your music without unlocking it—just double-tap the Home button and your Music app controls appear at the top of the screen.

Using iTunes Match to Back Up Your Other Songs to iCloud

When you turn on iCloud on your iPhone (see Chapter 9), turn on the iCloud backup, and run your first backup, it automatically backs up any music, books, or TV shows you've bought from the iTunes Store wirelessly to iCloud. However, it doesn't back up music you imported from CDs or bought somewhere else, but for around $25 a year, Apple offers a service called "iTunes Match." It searches your Music Library, finds which songs there are available in the iTunes Store, and when it finds a match, it adds it to your iCloud backup. So, what if it can't find some of your songs? Then, just upload those to iCloud yourself, and you're fully backed up. But it's not just the backing up of your songs that rocks about this— once it's set up, you can now stream your entire Music Library to any of your devices, so you always have access to it (and when it plays back, if the quality of your upload wasn't pristine, it streams it at high-quality 256-kbps AAC quality). How sweet is that? (I signed up for this as soon as it came out, and I love it!)

> **iTip** **Downloading Old iTunes Store Purchases from iCloud**
>
> *When you turn on iCloud, it backs up not only your iTunes Store purchases made on your iPhone, but also any purchases made on your other devices. To see all of your purchases, or just the ones not on your iPhone, tap the More button, then tap **Purchased** in the iTunes app. If a song (or book, or TV show) is not on your iPhone, you can download it by tapping on the little cloud icon with a down-facing arrow that's next to the song (book, TV show).*

Stream Music Wirelessly to Your Stereo Using AirPlay

All you need is either an AirPlay-compatible audio system (lots of companies make these, including JBL, Pioneer, Phillips, iHome, and B&W among others) or an Apple TV (it's not actually a television set, it's a very cool accessory you attach to your TV that lets you buy and rent movies and television shows, and a whole lot more), and then you're one tap away from streaming the music on your iPhone to your audio system. Here's how to use your iPhone's AirPlay feature: When you're playing a song, you'll see a button to the right of the volume slider (its icon looks like a widescreen TV with a triangle at the bottom); tap on that button and a list of any AirPlay-compatible speakers or Apple TVs you have connected appears. Tap on the set of speakers (or Apple TV) you want to have your music streamed to, and it starts streaming to those speakers (of course, you have to have the power on, on your AirPlay speaker system or Apple TV and home entertainment system, but you figured that, right?).

---

iTip   **Controlling Your AirPlay Music Using Apple's Remote App**

You can also use AirPlay to stream music wirelessly directly from iTunes on your computer, and if you're going to do that, you'll want to download Apple's free Remote iPhone app. It's like a remote control for your AirPlay devices right on your iPhone, so you can change songs, mute the sound, choose different AirPlay speakers, skip a song—you name it. You can find it in the App Store.

Shuffle Your Songs

By default, your Music app plays the songs in the order they appear in your playlists, but that can get really repetitive after a while, and it doesn't take long before you pretty much know which song is coming next. That's why the Shuffle (random) feature is so popular. Just go to the very top of any playlist, and tap on **Shuffle** (shown above), and now your Music app will pick and play songs in a random order. Also, if you're listening to a playlist without Shuffle turned on and decide you want to turn it on, you don't have to go digging through any screens, all you have to do is physically shake your iPhone back and forth, and Shuffle kicks in (it sounds weird until you try it, but it's actually kind of a fun, organic way to turn on a feature).

iTip **Shuffling When Your Phone Is Locked**

If your iPhone has gone to sleep while you're listening to your Music app, and you shake it, it won't shuffle because the phone is locked. But, there's a trick to get around that—just double-click on the Home button and the Music app controls appear (even though your phone is locked), and once you see those, you can shake to turn on the Shuffle feature.

Scrubbing Through a Song

The term "scrubbing" comes from the world of video editing, and it basically means that once a video is playing, you can grab the progress bar's slider knob and quickly move (scrub) it forward or backward through a video's timeline, seeing the video in fast speed as you move in either direction. The iPhone has this too, but your iPhone's scrubbing isn't just for video—you can scrub forward/backward through a song, podcast, audiobook, music video, etc., and you can not only go fast, but can also go very slowly and precisely if you want. You do this using the **progress bar** that appears onscreen (shown above circled in red) when a song or video is playing. If you tap-and-hold on the knob and drag left or right, you're in Hi-Speed Scrubbing mode (and it will say "Hi-Speed Scrubbing" right above the bar itself), but if you tap-and-hold on the knob and slide your finger downward, you'll see it change to Half-Speed, Quarter-Speed, and then Fine Scrubbing for very small movements.

Repeating a Song or Playlist

Start playing the song that you want to repeat or a song from the playlist that you want to repeat. There's a little **circular arrows icon** at the bottom left of the progress bar (circled above in red) that allows you to turn on Repeat. There are two modes to Repeat: Tapping the Repeat icon once will repeat the entire playlist after all the songs have been played. Tapping the Repeat icon again will show the circular arrows Repeat icon with a 1 on it. This means that the current song will repeat over and over until you stop it. Tap the Repeat icon one more time to turn Repeat off.

---

iTip **Playing Songs by Artist**

*If you're in the mood to hear some Evanescence but you didn't create a specific Evanescence playlist, just tap the Artists button at the bottom of the screen for a list of all your artists, then tap Evanescence. You'll see a choice between All Songs and their individual albums (if you only have one album for that artist, then you'll just see the songs). You'll see a list of albums even if you don't have all the songs on any of the given albums. You can tap **All Songs** to see a list of all the songs you have by that artist and then tap on a song to play them or you can tap a specific album to just play the songs on that album.*

Using Cover Flow

Cover Flow gives you a very cool, visual way of browsing through your music collection by seeing the album covers. To use Cover Flow, tap on the Music app. Once you're in the Music app, simply hold up your iPhone and turn it sideways in either direction. This will automatically switch the display to Cover Flow, and you now see your album cover art (or the music symbol, if a particular song doesn't have cover art). You can flick your finger across the screen to move through your albums. Once you find an album that you're interested in, tap on it and it will flip over to reveal the songs you have on that album. You can tap any song in that list to play it, and it will continue playing that album until it runs out of songs. To pause, press the tiny Pause button in the bottom-left corner of Cover Flow. To return to Cover Flow, tap the name of the album at the top, and the album flips back over and you're back looking at your album covers.

---

iTip **Another Way to Flip Albums**

You can also flip albums over and back by tapping the little **"i" button** in the lower-right corner of the Cover Flow screen.

Using Your Playlists

Playlists are groups of songs you create (like a collection of your favorite '80s rock songs, or music you've put together for a slide show, or your favorite songs for the road, and so on). You can create these playlists on your computer in iTunes (or right on your iPhone; see the next page), and then you choose which playlists get synced to your iPhone from iTunes (when you have your iPhone plugged into your computer, click on it in the Devices list on the left side of the iTunes window, then click the Music tab in the center. This is where you choose which playlists get copied over). To play the songs in one of these playlists, tap on the Music app, then tap on the **Playlists button** at the bottom of the screen to see your list of playlists. Tap on a playlist and it shows you the list of songs in that playlist. Tap on any song, and it will play the songs in just this one playlist in order.

---

iTip **You Can Have Loads of Playlists Without Taking Up Space**

The great thing about playlists is that you can have as many as you want without it eating up all of your iPhone's memory, because the same song(s) can be in multiple playlists without taking up additional space. For example, let's say you have a playlist called "Blues/R&B," one called "'60s music," and one called "My Favorite Janis Joplin Songs." All three playlists could contain Janis Joplin's "Ball and Chain" track, but that song will only be copied to your iPhone once, no matter how many playlists it's in. So, create as many playlists as you like—it won't affect your storage space.

Creating New Playlists

Your iPhone also has a Music app feature that lets you create regular playlists right within the Music app itself. Here's how it's done: Start by first tapping on the Playlists button at the bottom of the Music app screen, then tap **Add Playlist** at the top and a screen will appear asking you to name your new playlist. Type in a name, and tap Save. Once you tap it, you'll see a list of all your songs. Tap on the songs you want to add to your new playlist, and as you tap a song, the song's title turns gray to let you know it has been added. You can also tap on Playlists, Artists, or Albums to add songs that way. When you're done adding songs, tap the Done button in the upper-right corner and it displays the songs in your new playlist, it's added to your regular list of playlists, and you can create as many of these as you like. If you want to edit this playlist, just tap the Edit button in the top-left corner, and now you can delete a song by tapping the red – (minus sign) button to the left of the song's title, then tapping the red Delete button that appears to the right (if you change your mind, just tap the red – button again). To change the order of the songs, tap-and-drag the triple-line icon to the right of the song you want to move. You can add more songs by tapping the + (plus sign) button in the top-left corner of the screen. When you're done editing, tap the Done button at the top of the screen. If you want to start over, tap the Clear button at the top of the screen, then tap Clear Playlist, and it removes all the songs from the playlist. If you want to get rid if it, just tap the Delete button, then tap Delete Playlist.

Creating Genius Playlists on Your iPhone

If you're working out and this really great track comes on that gets you totally pumped, and you think to yourself, "I wish I had a playlist of more stuff like this," well, your Music app can automatically search through your songs and create a playlist based on that track you're listening to. You just tap on the **atom-looking icon** that appears below the progress bar of the song playing. Of course, you don't have to have a song playing to make a Genius playlist: just tap on the Playlists button at the bottom of the screen, then tap on **Genius Playlist** up at the top of the list, and it will bring up the list of songs in your Music app. For example, if I tapped on "Livin' on a Prayer" by Bon Jovi (hey, I like Bon Jovi) in my (Scott's) Music app, it would make a 25-song playlist and include songs like "Up All Night" by Slaughter, "Hysteria" by Def Leppard, "Signs" by Tesla, "Live Wire" by Mötley Crüe, and so on. By the way, once it has created a Genius playlist for you, it starts playing it right away, but if you tap the Back arrow at the top left of the screen, it'll not only display the songs in the Genius playlist, but it'll give you three buttons across the top: tap New to create a totally new Genius playlist; tap Refresh if you don't like the playlist it created and you want it to try again; or if you love that playlist and want to save it, tap Save. (*Note:* In order to use this feature, you must have the Genius feature turned on in iTunes on your computer. Once you sync your iPhone to your computer with the Genius feature enabled, you'll be able to create Genius playlists directly on your iPhone.)

Rating Your Songs on Your iPhone

While it's great that you can rate your songs as 1- to 5-star on your computer in iTunes, sometimes it's more convenient to rate songs right on your iPhone itself. To rate the currently playing song, tap the Track List button in the upper-right corner of the album art. The album art will flip over and you will see either **five dots** or the current rating that the song has. You can then tap the appropriate star/dot to rate your song as 1- to 5-star. Once you're done rating it, just tap the little Album Art button in the upper-right corner to return to your album art display. The next time you sync your iPhone to your computer, the ratings you made on your iPhone will be applied to those songs in iTunes on your computer (if you have this preference set).

---

iTip **Playing Other Songs from the Same Album**

To access songs from the same album as the song that is currently playing, start any song playing in the Music app that has at least two songs from the same album. Now tap the little Track List button in the top-right corner of the screen (to the right of the song's name). This will flip the album over and reveal the other songs that you have on that album. You can start playing any song you want on that list without having to go find it elsewhere.

Sing Along with the Lyrics

If you've taken the time to find the lyrics to your favorite songs, you can paste them into the Lyrics section for that particular song in iTunes on your computer (by clicking on the song in your Music Library, choosing **Get Info** from the File menu, and then clicking on the Lyrics tab). The next time you sync your iPhone, the updated song will be downloaded to it with the lyrics (if you have this preference set). To display the lyrics of a song that is playing on your iPhone, simply tap the album art that is currently displaying. To hide the lyrics again, just tap the lyrics, and they will go away and the album art will be displayed again.

Using the Audio Playback Control Widget

There's a built-in widget for quickly playing, pausing, rewinding, fast-forwarding, or controlling the volume of the music playing in your Music app, or audio streaming from the iTunes app (like an audio podcast) or other audio app (like Pandora). To get to this handy little widget anytime (no matter where you are in your iPhone), double-click the **Home button**, and the multitasking bar appears at the bottom of the screen. Now swipe to the right, and the control widget appears (seen above). Swipe to the right once more, and you'll see a volume slider. To control your music, tap the Play/Pause button, etc., then tap back anywhere on your screen area (basically, tap anywhere above the widget) to return to what you were doing, and your music continues to play in the background.

---

iTip Locking Your Screen Orientation

*That little control widget has an extra feature—if you tap the **circular arrow button** on the far-left side, it locks your screen in portrait (tall) orientation, so if you turn your screen sideways, it doesn't flip to a wide view like it normally would.*

Listening to Audiobooks

The iTunes Store has loads of audiobooks you can download, and you can buy them either on your computer or right on your iPhone itself. Unlike songs, the iPhone remembers right where you left off with an audiobook, whether you started listening to it in iTunes or on your iPhone, so you can listen in either place and the next time you sync to your computer, iTunes will update the audiobook to remember exactly where you left off (if you have this preference set). To listen to an audiobook on your iPhone, tap the More button at the bottom of the Music app screen, then tap **Audiobooks**. Now, tap the audiobook you want to listen to. The Next/Fast-Forward and Previous/Rewind buttons will advance you to the next chapter or take you back to the previous one. Also, you can change the speed of your audiobooks using the Playback Speed icon near the top right of the screen. More than likely, you'll use this to speed the audiobook up to double-speed (I wish they had a 1.5x speed), but you can also slow it down by tapping on it.

---

iTip Jump Forward or Back 15 Seconds for Audiobooks

If you're listening to an audiobook, near the top of the screen you'll see two circular arrows with a 15 in the center of them. If you tap on the left arrow, it jumps back 15 seconds. This is great if you need to take a note, or write down a web address that was mentioned and went by too quickly. If you tap the right arrow, it skips ahead 15 seconds.

Taking a Call While You're Listening to Music

If you receive a call while you're using the Music app, the sound will automatically fade and you'll hear your phone ring. The iPhone will give you the choice of answering the call or declining it (which will send the caller to voicemail). If you answer the call, then you'll be taken to the iPhone's call screen. Once you end the call, the iPhone will pick up right where it left off playing your song, video, audiobook, etc. If you're listening to music (or an audiobook, video, etc.) with the Apple headset that came with your iPhone, you can press the tiny **microphone button** on the right EarPod cable once to pause what's playing. To start playing it again, just press the button again.

Setting a Sleep Timer to Drift Off to Music

A sleep timer will play your music until the timer expires and then it will put the iPhone to sleep. To set a sleep timer, first go to your Music app and start playing the songs you want to play until the timer goes off. You can use a playlist (such as your "sleepy land" playlist—I know you have one—or any other playlist on your iPhone). Then press the Home button to go to the Home screen. Now tap Clock and then tap Timer. You can set the minutes, or hours and minutes, that you want the music to play before going to sleep. Next, tap the When Timer Ends button and choose **Stop Playing**. Then tap the Set button in the upper-right corner of the screen to return to the Timer screen. Now tap Start to begin the countdown. When the timer reaches the end of its set time, the music will fade out and the iPhone will go to sleep.

Rearranging Your Music Buttons

When you go to the Music app, you'll see buttons at the bottom of the screen for Playlists, Artists, Songs, Albums, and More. When you tap the More button, you'll see that you have more options (Audiobooks [if you have any], Compilations, Composers, and Genres). However, if you use any of these more often than the default buttons on the main Music screen, you can swap them. To move a button from the More screen to the main Music screen, tap the **Edit button** in the upper-left corner of the More screen. You'll then see buttons for all the Music app categories. Simply drag the button you want to move over the top of the button at the bottom that you want to replace with it, and when the existing button highlights, you can let go. When you've got the buttons you want in the order you want them, tap Done.

---

iTip **Moving Your Primary Music App Buttons**

While you're choosing which buttons you want to be your primary Music app buttons, you can also drag the ones that are there in a different order. For example, on my iPhone they are now listed as Artists, Playlists, Genres, Albums, and More. In the Configure screen, simply drag them in the order you want them listed.

Using External Speakers or Headsets

The dock connector on the bottom of your iPhone is similar to the dock connector on the bottom of a regular iPod, so you can connect your iPhone to an external speaker system made for an iPod. The new iPhone 5, though, uses a new connector on the bottom, called a Lightning connector (earlier iPhones use a 30-pin dock connector, which is the same as on earlier iPods and iPads). So, if you have a speaker system that has a traditional 30-pin connection, then you're going to need to use Apple's Lightning to 30-Pin Adapter to connect your iPhone 5. But, you can avoid all this and go wireless. Many new speakers, such as the iHome iW1 (shown above) and iHome iW2 speaker systems, are AirPlay enabled, so you can stream your music wirelessly to them. There are also Bluetooth speakers like the JAMBOX by Jawbone that work wirelessly via Bluetooth. The only downside to wireless speakers is that they don't charge your iPhone while in use, since you aren't docking it directly. But, in the case of the iHome iW1, there is a USB port on the back and you can plug your iPhone's USB cable into it to charge your iPhone while in use. Now, since the iPhone is a GSM-based phone, its built-in radio could interfere with your stereo or speakers. Turning on Airplane mode turns off the phone and Bluetooth portions of the iPhone, so it doesn't interfere with your stereo speakers. The only downside to this is that you won't be able to make or receive calls. That's why we recommend trying it with your speakers first, without going into Airplane mode, and if there's no interference, you're home free. Another way around this problem is to use Apple's iPhone 4 Dock, which has a stereo line out port that can be used to connect directly to your stereo system, and the adapter.

Chapter Eleven
Video Killed the Radio Star
Using the Videos App

 It's hard to believe, but the 1979 song "Video Killed the Radio Star," from The Buggles, actually has an important place in music history because when MTV went live back in August 1981, their debut music video was (you guessed it) "Video Killed the Radio Star." I have a regular iPod that does play video, but it doesn't have the larger, more luxurious widescreen display the iPhone has, and it was while pondering that thought, I realized the iPhone itself was playing a role in music history, and as an iPhone owner, like MTV, I would have to choose which music video would debut on my iPhone. Knowing that my choice would, in some small way, be part of my own personal music history really put a lot of pressure on me. I mean, think about it—years from now, it's quite possible that sociology students at colleges in far off places, like Helsinki (or Cleveland), might one day study, debate, and pick apart my music video debut choice, and I'm not sure I can deal with that kind of responsibility. And that's probably why, when I was carefully scrolling through my music video collection, rather than "flicking" or "swiping," I accidentally tapped the Play button right when the Spice Girls' "Wannabe" video was scrolling by, and I swear it felt like I went into some kind of slow motion dream state as I scrambled and fumbled to tap the Pause button…but it was too late. There it was, playing full screen. My only solace was, like The Buggles, the Spice Girls are British. If you listen carefully, you can almost hear the university professors in Helsinki giggling as they type their fall course descriptions.

Watching Videos on Your iPhone

You use the Videos app to watch movies, TV shows, and music videos on your iPhone that you can download from iTunes (on your computer) or the iTunes app (on your iPhone). To watch a video, just tap on the **Videos app**, tap on the video you want to watch, and it starts playing. The onscreen controls disappear after a few seconds, but if you want them back, just tap the screen and they reappear. For Hollywood movies, on iPhone 4S and earlier, most will appear in their original aspect ratio, which means you'll see them in let-terbox mode (with black bars at the top and bottom), but if you want to zoom them to full screen size, you can double-tap the screen—just know that the sides of the widescreen movie will be cropped off. The iPhone 5's screen is very much like the 16:9 ratio for HD, so if you download HD movies or TV shows, they will usually fill the entire screen without you having to zoom in. *Note:* If you shot video with your iPhone's built-in camera, those videos don't appear in the Videos app—they're in the Photos app, in your Camera Roll.

---

iTip **Watching Your Own Home Movies**

*You can convert your home movies in QuickTime format into the proper format right in iTunes (if it's not in the QuickTime format, see the iTip on page 221). Add the movie to your iTunes Library and choose **Create iPod or iPhone Version** from the Advanced menu.*

Buying Movies, Music Videos, and TV Shows

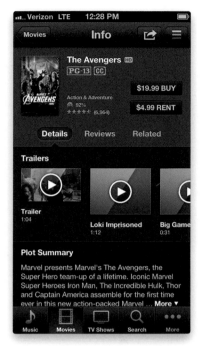

You can download videos (movies, TV shows, etc.) from the iTunes app directly on your iPhone without having to go to your computer first. Just tap the **Store button** in the upper-left corner of the Videos app (or tap on **iTunes** on your Home screen). You can buy or rent movies, and you can buy music videos and TV shows (video files are kinda large, so you'll need a Wi-Fi connection to download most videos from the iTunes app). The video is automatically synced back to your computer the next time you sync your iPhone with iTunes (if you have that preference set), so if you start watching on your iPhone, you can pick up in the same place on your computer (and vice versa). If you buy something, you'll be able to keep it and watch it as many times as you want. Movies that you rent will be available to start watching for up to 30 days. Once you start watching, you'll have 24 hours to finish watching it or to watch it as many times as you want within that time. Then, it will automatically delete itself.

---

iTip **What Happens When You Lose Wi-Fi During a Download?**

If you're downloading a video larger than 20 MB (so, just about any movie applies), you have to be on a Wi-Fi network to start your downloading process, but if you move out of range of your Wi-Fi connection, your iPhone will continue the download using its cellular network. Of course, it will take a lot longer, but at least it'll work.

Using AirPlay to Stream Video to Your Apple TV

If you have an Apple TV 2 or newer, you can actually stream video content wirelessly through your Apple TV so that you can enjoy it on the big screen. You have be on the same Wi-Fi network as your Apple TV. Then, just start your video playing and tap the little **AirPlay button** on the onscreen controls. You'll get a list of AirPlay-compatible devices, including your Apple TV, and once you choose it, the video will be playing on your TV instead of your iPhone. It's probably best to plug your iPhone into a power source if you're watching a long movie.

---

iTip **Deleting Videos on Your iPhone**

*You can delete videos directly from the iPhone to make more room. On the Video or episode screen, flick your finger across the title of the video to get a red **Delete button**. Tap it and the video is deleted from your iPhone immediately.*

Movie DVDs That Contain a Digital Copy

Some movie studios selling Blu-ray discs and DVDs include a digital copy (on a second disc) that is already formatted for your iPhone. It's the best of both worlds. You get a DVD or Blu-ray disc to watch on your big-screen TV, and you get a second disc that you put into your computer. Once you authorize the digital copy to your iTunes account, it's automatically copied into iTunes and is available to sync to your iPhone. The next time you're buying a movie on DVD or Blu-ray, be sure to check the packaging to see if it includes a digital copy. Some movie studios are including redemption codes for a digital download, instead, although these may require you to download a third-party app, such as Movies by Flixster (seen above), to watch the movie on your iPhone.

TiVo To Go

If you own a TiVo Series 2, Series 3, or TiVo HD, then you can transfer most of your recorded TV shows or movies from your TiVo to your computer using TiVo's TiVo-To-Go option. On a PC, there is a TiVo-To-Go app that you can download directly from TiVo's website (TiVo Desktop Plus software for PC). On a Mac, this functionality is available through Roxio's Toast Titanium software CD/DVD burning app. Once you have the TiVo-To-Go option set up, you can transfer unrestricted TV shows or movies directly from your TiVo DVR to your Mac or PC over your home network. Then, you can use the TiVo or Toast software to convert it to a format that will play on your iPhone. Depending on the size of the show (standard definition vs. HD), it could take several minutes or hours to transfer the content and convert it, so plan ahead.

---

iTip Set Your TiVo with Your iPhone

If you are a TiVo user, you can access most of the great features of the main TiVo website by going to their iPhone-friendly website using your iPhone's Safari app. Just go to m.tivo.com. Once you log in, it even remembers your password for you. It's a great way to schedule recordings while you're on the go! TiVo also has its own app that lets you control your DVR with your iPhone without interrupting the currently playing show.

Watching Videos Not Yet on Your iPhone

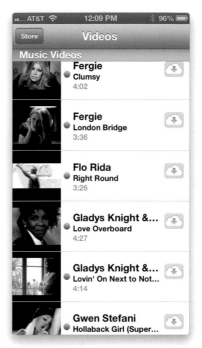

It's great that you can watch videos on your iPhone that you've synced from iTunes on your computer, or ones that you've downloaded from the iTunes app, but you can also watch videos that are in iTunes on your computer or music videos in iCloud before you actually put them on your iPhone. With Home Sharing enabled in both your Settings app's Videos app settings and your iTunes Preferences, you'll be able to access all of your iPhone-compatible videos via your Wi-Fi network. Just tap on **Shared** at the top of the Videos list and then choose any of the iTunes libraries running on your network that is logged into the same Home Sharing account. If you have an iTunes Match account and you have some music videos in iCloud, you'll be able to play/download those whenever you have an Internet connection, even if you're not at home. They will appear in your Videos list under Music Videos, with a cloud icon next to any of the ones that you haven't downloaded yet.

---

iTip **Watching Purchased DVDs**

iTunes doesn't convert regular movie DVDs that you purchased, like it does with CDs, but there is a workaround. Before I go any further, you'll have to check the laws in your country and the license agreements of the DVDs you've purchased to make sure that you aren't breaking any laws by converting them for your own personal use on another device, such as the iPhone. To convert a purchased movie DVD, you're going to need an additional program. My favorite one is called Handbrake. It's cross-platform, and, best of all, it's free! Remember, this process is for your own personal use only.

Chapter Twelve
One Hour Photo
Using Your Camera and Working with Photos and Videos

I chose the movie *One Hour Photo* as this chapter's title after realizing that my song title choices were pretty much either "Photos of Toast" by Ectogram or "Photos of Nothing" by Southeast Engine. I was leaning towards "Photos of Toast" until I heard "Photos of Nothing," and I knew right then I needed to find something more productive to do for a living other than searching the iTunes Store for songs that contain the word "photo." But I digress. I could have gone with two more obvious choices like "Photograph" from Ringo Starr or Def Leppard. Personally, I like Def Leppard's "Photograph," because I feel cooler lip syncing to them whilst holding a pool cue than I do when singing Ringo's song, which you want to avoid doing in any bar that has a pool table. Luckily that's not a big fear of mine because the odds of finding a jukebox with Ringo's "Photograph" on it (the one that starts with "Every time I see your face, it reminds me of the places we used to go. But all I've got is a photograph...") are less than winning the Powerball lottery. That's because Ringo just isn't very big with the pool hall crowd, which is, by the way, a crowd that does favor Def Leppard for one simple reason: Def Leppard is in the Pool Cue Air Guitar Hall of Fame. Sadly, it wasn't for "Photograph"—it was for "Pour Some Sugar On Me," which would have made a great chapter name if the iPhone had either Pouring or Sugar Dispensing features. Sadly, it has neither. I know what you're thinking, "He should have gone with 'Photos of Toast'." That's not what you were thinking, was it?

Using the Built-In Camera

To get to the camera, just tap the **Camera app** (shown circled above) and you'll see a full-color image of what you're pointing your iPhone at (the camera is on the back side of the iPhone, on the top left). A white square will appear briefly to show you what you're focusing on (more about this on the next page). To take a picture, tap the round button with a camera icon on it (the shutter button) at the bottom of the screen. You'll hear a shutter sound (like a regular camera), and then you'll see a graphic like a shutter closing and opening, so you know that it took the photo. If you have an iPhone 5 or 4S, you can actually use the Volume Up button on the side of your iPhone as your shutter button, as well. Once you take a photo, it's added to your Camera Roll (where all your photos are stored), and your camera is ready to take the next photo. If you want to quickly see the photo you just took, swipe to the right on the screen. To return to the camera, swipe to the left. To see the photos in your Camera Roll, tap the little square in the bottom-left corner of the screen.

---

iTip **Shooting Wide Photos**

If you want to shoot your photos in landscape (wide) orientation, just turn your iPhone sideways. To shoot in portrait (tall) orientation, just keep it turned upright.

How to Choose Where to Focus

Your iPhone has a built-in face detection feature, so if it sees a person's face in your photo, it automatically focuses on them, but if you want to it to focus somewhere else, you just tap on the thing you want it to focus on. That way, you can choose whether you want it to focus on something close, or something far. When you focus, a little white square appears onscreen to show you what the camera is focusing on. By the way, this "tap on what you want in focus" thing isn't just for focus. Where you tap is also the area the camera then uses to set the overall exposure for the photo and white balance, and this helps you get better-looking photos overall. One more thing: if something in your photo will be moving (like maybe a toddler, or your pet), then tap-and-hold for a moment. That locks the focus, so if they move, the focus doesn't jump over onto something else (more on this on page 232).

---

iTip   Shooting Over Your Head

Although we say "tap" the shutter button, sometimes it's better to press-and-hold the button until the moment you're ready to shoot. For example, if you're holding your iPhone up high (maybe over a crowd), it'll be hard to see right where to tap, so you might miss the shot. Instead, press-and-hold the shutter button while the camera is still right in front of you, and keep your finger held down on it as you raise up the camera. Then, to take the shot, you just remove your finger. This is also a great tip for taking self-portraits with the iPhone 3GS (since you can't see the screen).

Taking Self-Portraits

If you want to take a self-portrait (or a quick shot of you and a friend), you can use your iPhone's other camera (the one designed for doing FaceTime video calls). To turn on this second camera, just tap the **Camera Swap button** (the camera with circular arrows) in the top-right corner of the screen. When you do this, it shows you the view from the camera on the front of your iPhone. Just hold it out in front of you (you'll see a live preview onscreen) and then tap the shutter button (the round button at the bottom center of the screen with a camera icon on it) to take a photo of yourself. To switch back to the regular camera, tap the Camera Swap button again.

---

iTip   Seeing an Onscreen "Rule of Thirds" Grid

*To see a visible grid over your image (to help you compose your image using the photography "Rule of Thirds"), in the Camera app, tap on the Options button at the top of the screen, then tap on the **Grid OFF button** to turn it on, and then tap the Done button. This grid visually divides the scene into horizontal and vertical thirds—handy when you're trying to make sure your camera is straight when you're taking a landscape shot or a shot with a horizon line.*

Using the Built-In Zoom Feature

To zoom in on a particular area, just put your fingers together on the spot you want to zoom in on (like you're going to pinch something), then just spread them outward and it zooms in, and a **digital zoom slider** appears onscreen. Drag that slider to the right (toward the plus sign) to zoom in closer to your subject, and back to the left to zoom back out to normal. There is one thing you need to know about this zooming: it's digital zoom, rather than optical zoom, so the zooming is done in the software—the lens itself doesn't extend like a traditional camera lens. So, you lose a little picture quality when you zoom in digitally like this (this isn't just an iPhone thing—the same thing applies to regular HD video cameras that offer "digital zoom").

iTip **Going Straight from Your Camera to Facebook or Twitter**

*Once you've taken a photo, if you want to post it to Facebook or tweet it, just tap on the Camera Roll button (in the bottom-left corner of the camera screen), and then tap the button at the bottom of the screen with a square with an arrow coming out of it. Tap the **Facebook** or **Twitter button**, type your post or tweet, and when you tap Post/Send, your photo will automatically be attached and uploaded to Facebook or Twitter along with your text.*

Using the Built-In Flash

On the back of your iPhone 5, 4S, or 4, there's a small LED flash, and you can turn it on by tapping the **Flash button** (the button with the lightning bolt icon) in the top-left corner of the camera screen. This brings up a list of three flash options: (1) Off turns the flash off (I know, I didn't really need to explain that one); (2) Auto automatically turns the flash on if the camera senses it needs more light to make a decent picture; and (3) On turns the flash on whether you need it not.

---

iTip   Using Your Flash as a Flashlight

Shortly after the iPhone 4 came out with built-in flash, developers started introducing apps that let you keep the bright LED flash turned on, so you can use it as a flashlight (great for finding your car keys at night). There are a number of different flashlight apps out there, but the one I use is called Flashlight+, which sells for 99¢ (Terry picked it as his #1 pick for flashlight apps on his www .bestappsite.com, so I downloaded it right away and I love it).

Editing Your Photos Right on Your iPhone

You can do some key photo editing tasks right on your iPhone, like cropping, rotating, re-moving red eye, and enhancing the overall exposure of your photo. Tap on the photo you want edit in your Camera Roll (or other album), then tap the **Edit button** at the top right of the screen. This brings up a menu bar along the bottom of the screen. To rotate your image, tap the Rotate button (on the left). To automatically enhance the overall look of the photo, tap the Auto Enhance button (next to the Rotate button; it looks like a magic wand). Auto Enhance does a pretty amazing job in most cases, giving you more vibrant, colorful, and contrasty photos. The next button to the right (the round red circle with a line through it) is the Remove Red-Eye button. If you have a photo where someone has a red-eye reflection in their eyes, tap this button, then tap right on each eye to "get the red out." The last editing tool (on the right) is the Crop button. To crop your image, tap on it, then tap-and-drag your finger inward on any of the corners of the cropping border. If you want the photo to be a specific size, once you've resized the border, tap the Constrain button and choose a size. Then, you can reposition the photo within the border by just dragging it around with your finger.

---

iTip　**The Shortcut for Getting to Your Camera Fast**

If your iPhone is asleep, just click the Home button and a Camera button appears to the right of the Slide to Unlock button on the Lock screen. Flick upward on it and it takes you right to the camera, so you don't miss the shot.

Taking HDR (High Dynamic Range) Photos

Your iPhone camera has a built-in HDR feature that works wonderfully well in tricky lighting situations (like when part of the photo is really bright and part is really dark, which usually wreaks havoc on photos). When you turn this on (in the Camera app, tap on the Options button at the top center, then tap the **HDR OFF button** to turn it on), your camera automatically captures a wider range of exposure, which balances the light in the photo so it captures more detail. By default, when you take a photo with the HDR feature turned on, you take two photos: (1) the original photo, and (2) the HDR photo. Since they're right next to each other, you can swipe back and forth between them and keep the one that looks the best (you can delete the one you don't like by just tapping once on the Trash button at the bottom of the screen).

---

iTip My Favorite HDR App

If you're really into HDR photography, try my favorite HDR app, True HDR (available in the App Store for $1.99). I like to use its manual mode, where you first tap on the brightest thing in the image, then take a photo. Then, you tap on the darkest thing in the photo and take that photo. Then you tap the Merge button, and it aligns and combines the two images (one dark, one bright) into a single image with the best of both photos combined. I love it (and hope you will, too)!

Shooting Panoramic Photos

To shoot a panoramic photo (it looks like you shot a series of photos and stitched them together into one wide image, which essentially is what the iPhone 5 does for you), first turn your iPhone upright so that it's tall (it has to be vertical for you to take a panoramic photo). Now, tap on the Camera app, then tap on the Options button, and then tap the **Panorama button**. You'll see a horizontal bar appear across the center of your screen with an arrow facing right (as seen above left). To make a pano, tap the shutter button (the round button at the bottom of the screen), then move your iPhone horizontally from left to right, like you're taking a video of the scene in front of you. This works best if you keep your iPhone fairly straight and level while you do this. To help you do that, there's a solid line in the center of the bar and your job is to keep that arrow aiming right along that bar (try not to let it go below or above that line by either tilting your iPhone slightly toward you or away from you. This is much, much easier than it sounds). When you're done, tap the Done button at the bottom of the screen. Lastly, tap the small square thumbnail in the bottom left to see it. That is some amazing technology!

---

iTip   Starting Your Pano from the Right

By default, your iPhone is set up to shoot a panoramic image with you starting at the left and moving your iPhone to the right, but if you'd prefer to go the opposite way (from right to left), just tap on the white arrow in the horizontal bar and you're good to go.

Locking Your Exposure

If you're aiming your iPhone's camera at a scene and something looks really off (maybe the white is so bright it has turned white, or your subject is backlit and you can't see them at all—they're in the shadows), then just tap on different parts of the screen to see if you can find a better exposure (the overall brightness/darkness of your photos). Now, as long as you don't move your camera, you're set. But, what if you need to recompose the photo so it looks better? In that case, you can "lock" your exposure. Here's how: Go ahead and tap around on different parts of the scene until you find an exposure that looks good, then tap-and-hold on that area. After a moment or two, the square focus box will flash twice to let you know it has locked the exposure on that area and you'll see AE/AF Lock appear in small text at the bottom of your screen. Now, you can frame (compose) the photo any way you'd like and it will make its exposure based on where you locked it. To remove the lock, just tap once anywhere on the screen.

---

iTip   Apps for Editing Photos on Your iPhone

There are two apps I use on my iPhone that I think are amazing for editing your photos: (1) I use Camera+ when I want a quick, good-looking edit (try the Clarity button). And (2), if you want to take things a bit further and really create something amazing, then get Snapseed, from Nik Software. Apple named it the "iPad App of the Year" in 2011, and with good reason—it's like having Photoshop on your iPhone, but it's much easier to master.

Arranging Your Photos in Albums

Once you've taken a bunch of photos, you might want to arrange them into photo albums (like a Family album, or a Vacation album, and so on), so you can see groups of related images quickly with just one tap. To create an album, tap on the Photos app, and then tap the **+ (plus sign) button** in the top-left corner of the Albums screen, give your new album a name, and tap Save. Now your Camera Roll, Photo Library, Photo Stream (if you have it turned on; more about this on page 254), and a list of any other albums you've created will appear for you to find the photos you want to add to your new album. Tap on whichever album the photos are in, then tap on Select All Photos or tap each photo you want added (a blue circle with a checkmark will appear on each photo's thumbnail to let you know it has been selected). Once you've got all the photos you want selected, just tap the blue Done button (at the top right) and those photos will be added to your new album. To see it, just tap on it in your Albums list. To delete a photo from an album, just tap on it, then tap the Trash button at the bottom of the screen. Don't worry, this only removes the photo from that album, it doesn't delete it from your iPhone. To add more photos to that album later, go to your Camera Roll, tap the Edit button in the top right, tap on the photo(s) you want to add to select them, tap the Add To button at the bottom, and tap the Add to Existing Album button. This brings up the Add to Album screen, where you choose the album you want to add the photo(s) to. *Note:* You can only add photos to albums created on your iPhone.

Shooting Video with Your iPhone

The iPhone takes surprisingly good HD-quality video, and it couldn't be easier to use. Tap on the Camera app, and on the bottom right of the screen is a button where you choose between the still camera (the default choice) and the video camera. To shoot video, tap the button and it switches to video. Aim the camera where you want it, and if you need to focus on a particular person or object, tap the screen on that focus point (see page 225 on focusing). When you're ready to start recording your video, tap the button with the red dot at the bottom of the screen. You'll hear a "ding," and the red dot starts blinking to let you know you're now recording. You'll also see the length of the video next to the button. When you want to stop recording, tap the blinking red dot button and you'll hear two dings (and the red dot stops blinking). Once you're finished recording, to see your video, tap the small square thumbnail in the lower-left corner of the screen, then tap the Play button to see (and hear) your video. Also, just in case you were wondering, your video gets saved into your Camera Roll, right alongside your photos.

iTip	Muting the Shutter Sound When You Take a Photo

*If you're using your iPhone to take shots where you need to be quiet (like at a golf tournament, or a friend's wedding), you can lower the volume or mute the shutter sound altogether. While the Camera app is open, just use the **Volume buttons** or mute it using the **Ring/Silent switch** on the side of your iPhone.*

Shooting Video with Your iPhone Widescreen

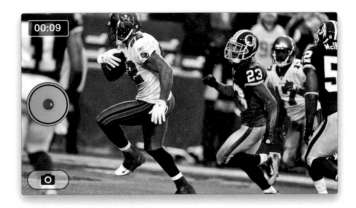

When you're shooting video, you'll probably want to turn your iPhone sideways, so you're shooting widescreen (like your TV). If you hold it straight up, you'll end up with a tall, skinny video (which kind of looks weird). Turning your iPhone sideways and shooting your video widescreen will give you larger videos, which are easier to see on your iPhone (or your computer, or TV).

---

iTip   **Seeing Which Thumbnails Are Video**

When you look on your Camera Roll screen, it's easy to see which thumbnails are photos and which are videos. The video clips have a small movie camera icon in the bottom-left corner of the thumbnail, and the length of the video clip, in minutes and seconds, is listed on the bottom right.

Editing Video on Your iPhone

If your video has some extra space at the beginning or end, you can trim it down to size right on your iPhone. In fact, you can pretty much just pick and choose which part of the video you want. Here's how: Find the video you want to edit in the Camera Roll (from the Home screen, tap on Photos), or if you want to edit the video you just shot, then tap the little square thumbnail in the bottom-left corner of the screen when you're done shooting. This brings up your video clip. Tap the screen and a Frame Viewer bar appears at the top of the screen. You can drag your finger along this bar to move to a particular part of the video clip. To trim your video to just the part you want, drag the left side of the **Frame Viewer bar** to where you want the video to start, then drag the right side of the Frame Viewer bar to where you want it to end. When you do this, the bar turns yellow, letting you know you're in Trim mode. Tap the Play button at the bottom of the screen to see your edited video clip. If you like it, tap the yellow **Trim button** at the top right, and it lops off that extra stuff on both ends, and now your video is cut down to size (so to speak).

---

iTip Deleting a Video

*If you want to completely delete a video, just tap on its thumbnail in the Camera Roll (so it appears full screen), then tap on the Trash button in the lower-right corner. When the menu appears, tap the **Delete Video button**.*

Video Straight from Your iPhone to YouTube

You can take video you've shot and publish it directly on YouTube.com right from your iPhone. Here's what you do: Once you've shot the video, tap on the thumbnail to bring it up full screen, and trim it down to the size you want (if necessary), then tap the Share button in the bottom-left corner of the video screen, and a menu will appear. Tap on **YouTube**, and your iPhone will compress the video and take you to the Publish Video screen (shown above), but before that screen appears, it's going to ask you to enter your YouTube.com username and password (you have to have a free YouTube account before YouTube will let you publish any videos there, so if you don't have an account, go to their website and sign up for one, or this is as far as you can go). Enter a title and description of your video, then add any tags (search terms), choose a category that matches your video, and choose whether you want it to be Public, Unlisted, or Private. Now you're ready to tap the Publish button at the top right of the screen and your iPhone will upload your video to your YouTube account. Once it's uploaded, a menu will appear telling you that your video has been published, with buttons for watching it right now on YouTube.com (from your iPhone), or sending a friend the link to the YouTube video, so they can watch it on their phone (or their computer). If you tap the Tell a Friend button, it copies-and-pastes the YouTube.com direct web link to your video into a new email message, and it puts the video's name as the subject line.

Your iPhone Treats Videos Like Photos

Well, that's pretty much true. Except for the fact that you can trim your video and send it up to YouTube.com, all the things in this chapter that pertain to working with photos on your iPhone also apply to video. For example, you delete a video the same way you delete a photo (tap on the Trash button). To see a photo or a video full screen, just tap on it. You can email a video just like you email a photo, and you can send a video in a text message just like you can send a photo, although you can't post it to Facebook, tweet it, or use the editing tools on it. You can even geotag videos just like you do photos (see page 240). You can choose where to focus the video camera, just like you do the still camera, and yes— it sets the video camera's exposure like that, too. So, you can pretty much figure, if you can do it to a photo, you can probably do it to a video, too!

---

iTip **Turn On the Flash for Shooting Video in the Dark**

If you have an iPhone 5, 4S, or 4, when you shoot video, your camera's flash turns into a continuous light, so you can have some light when you're shooting video in the dark. To turn on your video light, go to the Camera app, slide the switch over to video, then tap the **Flash button** *(the button with the lightning bolt) and choose On to light your video as you shoot.*

How to Shoot Stills While You're Shooting Video

That's right—you can do both! If you're already shooting video and decide you want to take a still image (without interrupting the video you're currently shooting), just tap the **Camera button** (shown circled in red above) and it takes a still. Each time you tap it, it takes another still. When you're done, these stills will appear right alongside your video in your Camera Roll.

Want to See Where You Took That Photo?

If you have Location Services turned on in your iPhone (go to the Settings app, tap Privacy, then tap Location Services, and turn it on. Also, make sure Camera is turned on in the list below), then your camera will automatically embed the GPS coordinates of where you took your photos as you take them. Some apps can actually show you on Google Maps where you were when you took the photo. Geotagging also places your photos on a world map on your iPhone. Just go to the Photos app and tap on **Places**. Little red pins on the map represent the places where you've taken photos or videos (you can pinch-and-slide your fingers outward to zoom in on the map). Tap on one of the pins, and it tells you how many photos and videos were taken at that particular place and shows you a thumbnail of the first one (as shown above). Tap the blue arrow, and it shows you thumbnails of all the photos and videos you took there. Also, if you upload your photos to Flickr.com, in the Flickr account preferences, you can turn on geotagging. Once it's turned on, photos from your iPhone will automatically appear on the map for your Flickr account.

iTip **Stopping the Auto-Rotation**

You know how when you turn your iPhone sideways, the screen automatically switches to a wide landscape view? Right, it's really handy, but what if you're looking at a photo, or showing somebody a photo, and you don't want it to automatically rotate? Just lightly press your finger on the screen, and now it won't auto-rotate, even if you turn it sideways.

Add Your iPhone's Geotag Info to Other Photos Using iPhoto

Each time you take a photo with your iPhone, it captures location information, and you can use that information to geotag photos taken with your regular digital camera (if it doesn't have GPS). First, take a picture with your iPhone, then put it away and start shooting with your regular camera (be sure to shoot one photo with your iPhone each time you move to a different location). Import both your iPhone and your regular digital camera shots into iPhoto (which comes preinstalled on all new Macs). Select the first iPhone shot from the first location, Right-click on it, and choose Copy. Now select all the other photos from the same location, and from the Edit menu, choose **Paste Location**. iPhoto will then add the longitude and latitude location info to all the other photos. Just rinse-and-repeat for the rest of the shots from your shoot.

---

iTip   **Tag Your Photos with Faces**

If you're a Mac user and you import your photos into iPhoto or Aperture, you can tag your photos with Faces and those groups of photos will appear when you tap the Faces button in the Photos app.

If You Shoot Video, Get iMovie for iPhone

Although you can do some simple video editing right on your iPhone (like trimming the length), you can't add background music, or titles, or combine multiple clips, or any of the other cool things you can do with Apple's iMovie app (just $4.99 from the App Store, but worth much more). This is an iPhone version of Apple's popular iMovie for the Mac, and it's really amazing what they've done with it—you can give your videos a slick, produced look, all from the palm of your hand. Here's how it works: Launch iMovie and tap the **Tap + to Start a New Project or Trailer button** to start a new project. Choose one of their built-in themes (these pro-designed templates are what give your video that pro-quality look) and if you want, turn on Theme Music. Next, choose whether you want to use some video you've already shot or if you want to shoot something new (if you shoot something new, it'll automatically add a smooth fade between your video clips). Once your clips appear at the bottom of the screen, double-tap on any one of them to bring up the Clip Settings menu, where you can choose a Title Style for your theme (if you leave this set to None, you won't see the theme when you play your video), add some text, and make changes to your location and audio settings. To see a preview of your movie, tap the Play button. To see your full project, tap the star-on-a-page icon in the top left, and it takes you to a list of all your projects, and you can now see it full screen (by tapping the Play button at the bottom of the screen). Once you've completed your masterpiece, you can easily share it to your Camera Roll (for email and MMS), YouTube, Facebook, Vimeo, iTunes, and even CNN iReport (by tapping the icon with the arrow coming out of the box—you get to choose your final size at this point). Try it once, and you'll be a mini-moviemaker forever.

Getting Photos into Your iPhone (Mac)

If you're using a Mac, the easiest way to get photos into your iPhone is using Apple's iPhoto application (which comes pre-installed on all Macs). You drag-and-drop your photos right onto the iPhoto icon in your Mac's onscreen Dock and it imports them into your iPhoto Library. Then, click on the Create button near the bottom right to create separate photo albums (like one for family shots, or one for travel photos, one for your portfolio if you're a serious photographer, etc.), and drag-and-drop photos from the Library right onto the album of your choice. Once your photos are arranged in albums within iPhoto, when you connect your iPhone to your computer, iTunes automatically uploads your photo albums to your iPhone (if you have this preference set), or you can choose which albums to upload. You can see your uploaded albums by going to the Photos app.

---

iTip **Uploading Specific Photo Albums**

*You can set up your iPhone so only certain iPhoto albums are uploaded to it. You do this in iTunes when your iPhone is connected to your computer. On the left side of the iTunes window, under Devices, click on your iPhone to bring up its preferences. Click on the Photos tab, then turn on the Sync Photos From checkbox, and choose iPhoto from this pop-up menu. You'll see that the default setting has all of your iPhoto albums being uploaded. To choose just specific albums to be uploaded, click on the **Selected Albums, Events, and Faces, and Automatically Include radio button**, then turn on the checkboxes beside the albums, events, and faces you want uploaded. When you're done, click the Apply button in the bottom right.*

Getting Photos Without iPhoto (Mac)

If you don't want to use Apple's iPhoto application to manage the photos you want uploaded to your iPhone, you can just put them in a folder on your Mac and then upload them through iTunes. Here's how: First, connect your iPhone to your computer, which brings up iTunes (if you have this preference set). In the Source list on the left side of the iTunes window, under Devices, click on your iPhone to bring up the iPhone preferences, then click on the Photos tab. At the top of this pane, turn on the Sync Photos From checkbox, and from this pop-up menu, select **Choose Folder**. This brings up a standard Open dialog, where you choose which folder your photos are in. Once you navigate your way to that folder, click the Open button, then go to the bottom-right corner of the iTunes window and click the **Apply button** to upload the photos in that folder to your iPhone. If you have photos in subfolders, they will show up as individual albums on your iPhone, and you can choose which of these subfolders are uploaded by clicking on the Selected Folders radio button near the top of the Photos pane, and turning on the checkboxes for only the subfolders you want on your iPhone. Easy enough.

---

iTip   Finding the Number of Photos in an Album

If you're looking inside an album on your iPhone, and want to know how many photos are in it without having to return to the main Albums screen, just scroll all the way to the bottom of the thumbnails and you'll see how many photos are in that album.

Getting Photos into Your iPhone (PC)

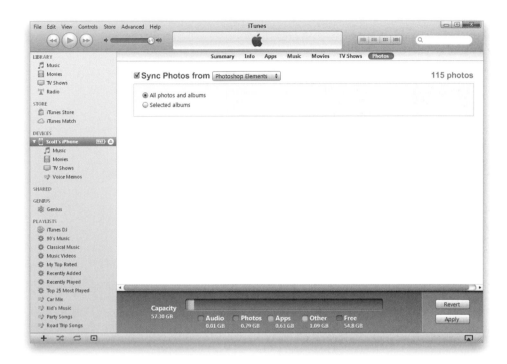

There is no version of Apple's iPhoto application for Windows, but your iPhone does support direct automatic importing from two other photo management applications: (1) Adobe Photoshop Album version 2 (which was a free application that Adobe offered, but has since discontinued). Or (2) any version of Adobe Photoshop Elements since version 3. To set this up, first connect your iPhone to your computer, which brings up iTunes (if you have that preference set). In the Source list on the left side of the iTunes window, under Devices, click on your iPhone to bring up the iPhone preferences, then click on the Photos tab. At the top of this pane, turn on the Sync Photos From checkbox, and from this pop-up menu, choose which one of the two supported applications you want to import from—Photoshop Album or Photoshop Elements. Now click the **Apply button** in the bottom-right corner to upload the photos to your iPhone. If you have albums set up in Elements, you can click on Selected Albums and turn on the checkboxes for the albums you want on your iPhone.

---

iTip Changing the Order of Your Photos

To change the order of your photos, you have to go back to your computer. Change the order the photos appear in the album, then go to iTunes, sync your iPhone with your computer, and it will update your iPhone with the new order.

Getting Photos Without Album or Elements (PC)

If you don't want to use Photoshop Album or Photoshop Elements to manage the photos you want uploaded to your iPhone, you can just put them in a folder on your PC and then upload them through iTunes. Here's how: First, connect your iPhone to your computer, which brings up iTunes (if you have that preference set). In the Source list on the left side of the iTunes window, under Devices, click on your iPhone to bring up the iPhone preferences, then click on the Photos tab. At the top of this pane, turn on the Sync Photos From checkbox, and from this pop-up menu, select **Choose Folder.** This brings up the Change Photos Folder Location dialog (it's like a standard Open dialog), where you choose which folder your photos are in. Once you've made your way to that folder, click the Select Folder button, then go to the bottom-right corner of the iTunes window, and click the **Apply button** to upload the photos in that folder to your iPhone. If you have subfolders in that folder, you can also click the Selected Folders radio button near the top of the Photos pane, and turn on the checkboxes only for the subfolders you want to upload. The subfolders will show up as albums on your iPhone.

iPhone Tips for Photographers

If you're a professional photographer or serious hobbyist, you've probably already figured out that the iPhone makes for a great tool to show off your shots. However, there are some other ways you can use the iPhone to help you with your future shoots. First of all, since the iPhone can have multiple albums, you can have multiple portfolios on hand to show friends, family, and prospective clients. You can also use the iPhone to display different lighting setups that you shot, as well as shots you'd like to do. You might also consider an album of various poses. This way, you can walk right over to your model and show them exactly how you'd like them to pose without them having to leave the set and walk over to your computer. The possibilities are endless. Just sync these albums from your computer to your iPhone the next time you connect them.

Viewing Your Imported Photos

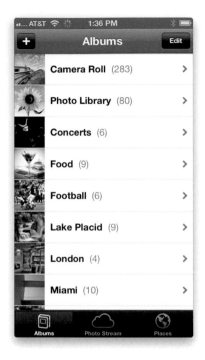

Once you've imported photos into your iPhone, to see them, tap on the **Photos app**. This brings up the Albums screen and at the top is your Camera Roll (the photos taken with your iPhone's camera), then your Photo Library (all the photos you've imported into your iPhone all lumped together), and then a list of any separate photo albums, like family photos, vacation photos, etc., you created on your iPhone or your computer. To see your photos as thumbnails, tap on any album. You can scroll through your thumbnails by swiping your finger up/down the screen. To see any photo full screen, just tap on it. Once your photo is full screen, you can see other photos in that album at that size by swiping your finger on the screen in the direction you want to scroll. If your photo bounces like it's hitting a wall, you've reached the end of that album, so swipe back in the other direction.

---

iTip **Deleting Multiple Photos from Your Camera Roll**

To delete multiple photos from your Camera Roll (to delete photos from your Photo Library or individual photo albums, you'll have to re-sync your iPhone), first tap the Edit button in the top-right corner of the screen, then tap on the photos you want to delete (a red circle with a checkmark will appear on the thumbnail to let you know it's selected), then when all the ones you want to delete are selected, tap the red **Delete button** in the bottom-right corner.

Viewing a Slide Show

 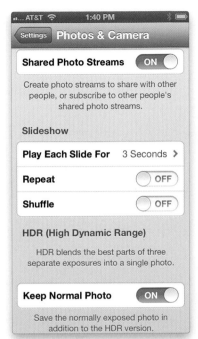

To see a slide show of your photos, tap on the Photos app to bring up the Albums screen. To see any photo album as a slide show, just tap on the album, then when the thumbnails appear, tap on one, then tap the **Play button** at the bottom of the screen. The slide shows come complete with smooth, built-in dissolve transitions between each photo, but you can choose a different type of transition on the Slideshow Options screen that appears when you tap the Play button. You can also add music here (we'll cover that next). When you're ready, tap the **Start Slideshow button**. To stop your slide show, just tap the screen once. To change the length of time each photo appears onscreen, go to the Settings app, and tap on **Photos & Camera**. Here you also have options for Repeat (to loop your slide show) and Shuffle (to play your slides in a random order). When you're done, tap the Settings button in the upper-left corner.

---

iTip **Emailing Multiple Photos**

*Emailing more than one photo at a time is pretty much the same process as deleting multiple photos (see the iTip on the previous page), except it works in all your photo albums. Once the photos are selected (up to five maximum), tap the Share button, then tap the **Mail button**. Note: If you select too many, the Mail button disappears (you'll only get the Message button, where you can send up to 9 photos), so tap on any selected photo to deselect it.*

Adding Background Music to Your Slide Show

To add background music to your slide show, in the Photos app, tap on the album you want to view, then tap on a photo in the album, and then tap on the Play button at the bottom center of the screen. On the Slideshow Options screen that appears, tap on the **Play Music OFF button** to turn it on, then tap on the Music field that appears. This brings up your Songs list from your Music app. Just pick a song, then tap the Start Slideshow button. Your slide show will begin, and so will the music.

---

iTip Pausing Your Slide Show

*To pause a running slide show, just **tap the screen**. To start it running again, tap the Play button at the bottom center of the screen, then tap the Start Slideshow button.*

Viewing and Saving a Photo/Video Sent in a Text Message

If someone sends you a photo in a text message (see Chapter 3 for more on texting), you'll see a thumbnail of the photo appear in your Messages conversation. Just **tap on it** to see it full-screen size. If you decide you want to save this photo on your iPhone, tap on the full-screen photo, then tap the button in the top-right corner, and then tap the **Save to Camera Roll button**, and it's saved to your iPhone's Camera Roll.

---

iTip   Copying-and-Pasting Photos

When you're looking at a photo at full-screen size, you can copy that photo into memory in case you want to paste it into another app (like an email message, or text message, etc.) by pressing-and-holding on the photo for a moment or two, and the word "Copy" will appear. Tap on that to copy the current photo into memory. Now you can paste it wherever you want (well, wherever you can normally paste stuff, anyway).

Making a Photo Your iPhone's Wallpaper

When you wake your iPhone from sleep, or when you're making a call, you can have a photo appear as your background image. To do this, tap on the Photos app, and when the Albums screen appears, tap on the album that contains the photo you want to use as your background wallpaper. Then, when you see the thumbnails screen appear, tap once on the photo you want to use, then tap on the button in the bottom-left corner of the screen and a list of options pops up. Tap the **Use As Wallpaper button**, and a new screen appears where you can adjust the size and position of your photo by tapping-and-dragging it around on the screen and pinching out to zoom in on the photo. When it looks good to you, tap Set, and then tap Set Lock Screen (or tap Set Home Screen to make it your Home screen wallpaper).

---

iTip | **Zooming In on a Photo**

To get a closer look at any photo, either in your photo albums or a photo you've taken with the built-in camera, just tap on the photo thumbnail to see it full screen, then place your pinched fingers in the center of the screen and spread them outward to zoom in (or just double-tap on the screen). To zoom in tighter, pinch-and-spread outward once again. To return to the normal-sized view, just double-tap on the screen.

How to Email a Photo

There are two ways to email a photo: (1) from the Mail app, or (2) from the Photos app (let's start with #1). Tap on the Mail app, then tap the New Message button. Double-tap in the message body, and then tap on the right-facing arrow in the pop-up menu. Tap **Insert Photo or Video** and this bring up your Photos app. Find the photo you want to email, tap the Choose button, and it's inserted into your email. To email a photo from the Photos app, tap on the Photos app, then find and tap on the photo you want to email. When the selected photo appears at full-screen size, tap the button on the bottom-left corner of the screen and tap on the **Mail button**, which takes you to the New Message screen and you'll see that your photo is already included at the bottom of the email. Enter the email address for the person you're sending the photo to in the To field, then tap the Send button in the upper-right corner of the screen. When you tap Send, you'll get a menu that asks you what size you want to send the file (larger sizes take longer to email). Choose your size, and away it goes.

Access Your Photos from Anywhere Using iCloud

Apple's iCloud can automatically take the photos you've taken with your iPhone and send them wirelessly to all your other devices (like your iPad, your computer, and so on). That way, your images are on all your devices all the time (how cool is that?). No more, "Oh, I wish I could show you that, but it's on my iPad" (or iPhone, or computer), because now you'll have them everywhere. Photo Stream is included in iCloud's free service. Here's how to set it up: Tap on the Settings app, then scroll down and tap on iCloud. Enter your Apple ID, then switch on **Photo Stream**, and now the photos you take with your iPhone will be sent wirelessly to all the devices you have iCloud turned on for. There's more to iCloud than just this, so make sure you read the iCloud chapter (Chapter 9) to learn more about accessing your photos with iCloud and all the other cool things iCloud can do.

---

iTip   Your Camera Can Get Really, Really Close

Your iPhone's camera has an automatic macro feature for taking really close-up photos. In fact, it will focus up to just a few inches from the object you're trying to shoot (you can get as close as 4" away). You may be thinking, "Why would I want a photo taken that close to anything?" Actually, it's fun (you just have to try it for yourself). Go ahead and try it right now—grab your iPhone, tap the Camera app, get around 4"–5" from something, and you'll see that the macro auto-focus kicks right in. I know. It's cooler than it sounds.

Downloading Photos from Your iPhone

Although you can use iTunes to manage just about everything on your iPhone, when it comes to your iPhone's camera, you treat it just like you would any other digital camera—when you connect it to your computer, if it has photos on it that you've taken, whatever software you have installed to import photos will likely launch. For example, if you're a Mac user, chances are iPhoto or Image Capture will launch and offer to import your shots. If you're a Windows user, the AutoPlay dialog or Windows Camera Wizard will kick in. You're not limited to these apps, though. You can use Photoshop Elements, Photoshop Lightroom, Apple's Aperture, Adobe Bridge's Photo Downloader, Windows Photo Gallery, or just about any other app that can bring images in from a camera. If you just want to download the images you've taken to a folder on your computer, then you can use Image Capture on your Mac or AutoPlay on your Windows PC. Both of these apps will download the images you've taken with your iPhone to a folder of your choice. From there you can do whatever you'd like with them, as they are regular JPEG files. (*Note:* You can also download them wirelessly using iCloud, as mentioned on the previous page.)

Chapter Thirteen
Cereal Killer
Killer Tips and Tricks

 This is the sixth edition of this book, and anytime we get a chance to update a book, we want to do more than just update the book with the new features—we want the new book to be better than the previous versions, because apparently we have something terribly wrong with how our brains are wired. You see, most authors are content with just updating their books, but Terry and I look at those other authors, who have things like a family life, and friends, and free time, and successful careers outside writing, and we say to ourselves, "Look at those suckers. They're out there having fun and enjoying their families when they could be indoors, tied endlessly to their laptops, typing on a keyboard, until they have nothing but bloody stumps where their fingers used to be." We laugh and poke fun at these "fun-loving" authors because clearly, they're just not "committed" enough to risk their marriages, jobs, and the occasional felony charge to really take their books to the next level. So, when Terry came up with the idea to add this chapter, even though we had already finished all the writing and updating, and the book was due to go to press, as you might imagine, it added some stress. Now, you know and I know how harmful stress can be to your health and well-being. In fact, many unlicensed physicians now feel that anxiety from writing extra tips like this can lead to stress-related health problems—in particular, cardiovascular problems that increase your risk of strokes and heart attacks—which is precisely why we named this chapter "Cereal Killer," after the song by Method Man and Redman. We considered the name "Death Trip," but only in passing.

Slide a Push Notification Icon to Go to That App

If you receive a push notification on your Lock screen, instead of using the usual Slide to Unlock feature, try sliding the icon for the app delivering the push notification to unlock your iPhone and go right to that app all at the same time. This is also useful for Passbook notifications to bring up the Passbook pass for the business that you're near.

Send a Tweet or Post a Facebook Status from the Notification Center

One of the fastest ways to post a Facebook status update or send a tweet is to do it from the Notification Center. Just swipe down from the top of any screen to bring up the Notification Center, and from there you can **Tap to Tweet** to Twitter or **Tap to Post** a Facebook status update. You'll get a page screen that allows you to key in your post or tweet for the respective social media sites. Keep in mind that, for these options to be available, you will need to first sign in to Twitter or Facebook in the Settings app.

Get Notified When You Receive an Email from a VIP

I personally do not want my iPhone alerting me every time I receive an email—that would drive me insane. So, I always have Mail turned off in my Notifications settings. If I want to check my email, I'll just go the Mail app. However, for those of you out there who find it important to be alerted when an email comes in from a particular person or group of people, you're in luck! Since iOS 6 now includes a VIP designation for email, you can actually turn on VIP alerts in the Notifications settings, so you'll only receive alerts when you receive email from people that you've designated as VIPs. Just tap Notifications in the Settings app, scroll down and find Mail, and tap on it (if you don't have Mail in your Notification Center yet, just tap the Edit button at the top right, tap-and-hold on the three lines to the right of Mail, and drag it up into the In Notification Center section). You'll see your email accounts listed on the Mail screen and you can turn on or off the notifications on an account-by-account basis. However, if you scroll down to the bottom, you'll see **VIP**. Tap on it, and you can set the type of notifications you want for any email received from your VIPs. This is great for when you want to know about those important emails from the boss or family, but you don't want to be alerted by a sale at your favorite drug store.

Restrict Access to a Single App

Your iPhone has a lot of personal information in it, so chances are you cringe a little when someone asks to use your iPhone. Sure, you don't mind them using it, but you don't want them snooping around in your apps, such as Mail and Messages. Here's a trick that allows you to limit access to a single app (the one that you/they want to use): in the Settings app, tap on General, and then scroll down and tap on Accessibility. Scroll down again, tap on **Guided Access**, and then turn it on. Now, tap on Set Passcode and enter a passcode. Once your passcode is set, go into the app that you want them to use, and triple-click the Home button to turn on Guided Access for that app only. Now they can only use that app until you triple-click the Home button again and enter your passcode.

Refresh Your Passbook Balance

When you add a card to Passbook, such as your Starbucks card or your AMC Stubs card, they display balances, and these balances will eventually automatically update. However, there is a way to update the balance for a particular card when you want to. Just bring up the card you want to refresh in Passbook, then tap the **"i" button** in the lower-right corner. This will flip the card over, where you will see the details about it. Now, swipe down on the screen to refresh the card. This will cause the card to check your account on the spot and update the balance.

Take Safari into Full-Screen Browsing Mode

There's a slightly hidden Safari feature in iOS 6: If you turn your iPhone sideways while you're in Safari, you will see a **double arrow button** at the right end of the bottom toolbar. Tapping this will take the current site you're viewing into full screen mode, hiding the URL bar and the toolbar. Basically, this will maximize your webpage to take advantage of the entire screen on your iPhone. To go back to the normal screen mode, just tap on the double arrow button that appears in the bottom right of the screen.

See Your Safari Browsing History

By now, we all know that when you tap a link on a webpage in Safari and it takes you to another page, tapping on the Back button will take you back to the previous page. However, in iOS 6, you can tap-and-hold the **Back or Forward buttons** to bring up your Back or Forward browsing history. This makes it much easier to get back to a page that was several pages back, rather than having to hit the Back button multiple times, or to go forward if you've gone back a couple pages.

Use Safari to Upload Photos

When you go to a website that you want to upload a photo to, perhaps to update your profile picture, you no longer have to wait until you get back to your computer. In iOS 6, you can use Safari to update a picture directly on the site you're browsing. Go ahead and tap the Upload or Attach button on the site, and Safari will give you the option to take a new picture with your iPhone camera or upload one from your Camera Roll or Albums.

Mirror What's on Your iPhone to Your Apple TV

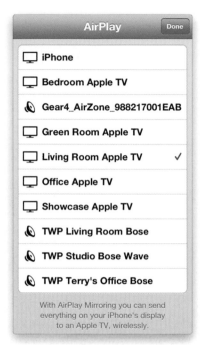

If you've got an iPhone 5 or 4S and an Apple TV 2 or newer with the latest software up-dates, you can actually mirror your iPhone's display to your Apple TV and the big screen. This is great for showing apps to a large audience or doing demonstrations. While some apps support AirPlay natively, most don't, but now you can show virtually any app on your TV. Make sure your iPhone is on the same Wi-Fi network as your Apple TV and then double-click the Home button and swipe the task bar to the right twice. This should reveal both the volume slider and the AirPlay button. Tap the AirPlay button, choose your Apple TV, and tap the **Mirroring button**, and then anything you do on your iPhone should be shown on your TV. When you want to turn it off, just double-click the Home button again, swipe to the right twice, tap the AirPlay button, and choose iPhone.

Set Up a Custom Vibration Pattern

You can create custom vibrations and assign them to contacts, which is useful if you can't really tell if your iPhone is vibrating when in Silent mode, or if you want it to vibrate a certain way when a specific person calls. In the Settings app, tap on Sounds, then tap on Ringtone, and at the top, you'll see Vibration. Tap on the current vibration setting, and near the bottom, under Custom, tap on **Create New Vibration**. On this screen, just tap out the vibration pattern of your choice, and tap the Stop button. Tap the Play button to make sure it's what you wanted, or tap the Record button to try again, and once you're happy with the one you created, tap the Save button to give it a name and save it. Now, you'll be able to change your default Vibration pattern in your Sounds settings, as well as assign custom vibration patterns to contacts in their Contacts Info screens.

---

iTip **Assign a Contact a Vibration Pattern of None**

*Even if you turn your ringer to Silent, you'll still get vibration alerts for phone calls. If you know you get calls or text messages from a business, like reminders from your bank or doctor, and you don't want your iPhone to vibrate when they come in, you can assign a contact a Vibration pattern of None. In the contact's Info screen, tap on Edit in the top right, scroll down and tap on Vibration, and then scroll down and tap on **None**.*

Use Your iPhone to Dictate into Other Apps

With an iPhone 5 or 4S, you can ask Siri questions and get answers back. You can also use the speech recognition of the iPhone to dictate messages or text in other apps. If you're in an app and you see a microphone icon on your keyboard (to the left of the Spacebar), then you can tap the microphone icon and start talking instead of typing. While the iPhone is pretty good at speech recognition, it doesn't automatically punctuate. You'll actually have to say the word "period" at the end of a sentence to have your iPhone add a period. Also, it works best in small bits, instead of trying to dictate long paragraphs. When you're done dictating, tap the Done button to see how well it did.

Cut, Copy, Paste, Suggest, and the Landscape Keyboard

Double-tap on a word and you will get blue grab points to select what you want to copy—this can also include images, say from an email or webpage in Safari. If you double-tap where there is no word or tap-and-hold your finger on the screen for a few seconds, you'll get a different menu that allows you to Copy, Select (using the grab points), or Select All. Once the area you want to copy is selected, tap the Copy button. Go to the app that you want to paste this info into, double-tap (or tap-and-hold) where you want to paste it, and then just tap the Paste button. You can also replace words. Just double-tap on a word and, in the menu, you'll see a Suggest button if there are other words that your iPhone thinks you might want to use. Tap Suggest and then tap on the word you want to use instead. One other important feature: you can turn your iPhone sideways to get a landscape keyboard in most of your built-in apps such as Mail, Messages, and Notes.

---

iTip **Copying-and-Pasting Photos**

*You can also copy-and-paste photos from the Photos app. Just go to the photo you want to copy and tap the box with the arrow coming out of it in the bottom-left corner of the screen, and then tap the **Copy button**. Now, just switch to the app you want to paste the photo(s) into, double-tap on the screen, and then tap the **Paste button**.*

Master the Virtual Keyboard

When you first type on your iPhone keyboard, you'll probably want to fix your mistakes as you type, but the iPhone is smart and fixes most mistakes automatically. It compares what you're typing to the adjacent keys and usually guesses the right word, so keep typing. If you did make a mistake that you wish to fix, you don't have to delete the whole word. Tap-and-hold over the word and a magnifying glass appears. You can now slide your finger over to move the cursor to where you want to make your change or deletion. If you start typing a word that is familiar to the iPhone, it may offer a suggestion. If the suggestion is correct, hit the Spacebar; if it's wrong, keep typing. If you see a red underline, tap on the word to get suggestions. When you finish a sentence, there is no reason to hit period and then the Spacebar. If you double-tap the Spacebar, the iPhone will insert a period and a space, as well as enable the Shift key for the next sentence. By default, you can double-tap the Shift key to turn Caps Lock on and tap it again to turn it off.

---

iTip **Turning Auto-Correction Off**

*You can turn off the iPhone's corrections by going to Settings, tapping on General, tapping on Keyboard, and then turning **Auto-Correction** off.*

Access Those Special Accent Characters

The next time you need to type an accent character, simply tap-and-hold on the key that would have the accent and the available accent characters will pop up. Slide your finger over to the character you want until it highlights, and then take your finger off the screen. Additional special characters are also supported. For example, if you tap-and-hold the period key, you'll get the option to insert an ellipsis (…).

---

iTip | Turning Off the Keyboard Clicking

*As I'm sure you've heard, the iPhone keyboard makes a clicking sound as you type, similar to that of a classic typewriter. Although I prefer to have this sound off completely (you can turn it off in the Settings, under **Sounds**), I know several people who like it. However, if you need to silence it temporarily, say in a meeting, then just turn your ringer off by moving the **Ring/Silent switch** (near the top on the left side of your iPhone) to Silent mode (move it toward the back of your iPhone).*

Switch to a Foreign Language Keyboard

To have access to multiple foreign language keyboards and be able to switch between them whenever you want, you first have to choose the ones you'll want to use. To do this, tap on the Settings app, then tap General, then tap International, then tap Keyboards, and then tap **Add New Keyboard**. This screen lists all the languages you can choose from. Tap on the keyboard(s) you want, and now when you're in an app where you need to type something, you'll see a little globe button on the bottom left of the keyboard. Just tap-and-hold on that button to switch between the keyboards you've turned on.

Want to Use Emoticons?

If you want to add a little graphic flavor to your text and email messages, you can enable the built-in Emoji keyboard. You turn this keyboard on in your Settings app, in the General settings. Tap on International, then tap on Keyboards, tap on Add New Keyboard, and then scroll down and tap on **Emoji**. Once you enable it, there will be a globe icon at the bottom left of your keyboard. You can now switch between your native language keyboard and the Emoji keyboard by tapping the globe icon whenever you want to use the built-in emoticons. Tap on the buttons along the bottom to change categories, and swipe to the left to see more in that category. While it's great that we can use these, you have to keep in mind that not all operating systems will display them properly. It's probably best to stick to using these when you know you're texting another iOS user.

Tips for the International Traveler

While you might have an unlimited data plan at a set price with your carrier, all bets are off when you travel outside your country. Data roaming charges can be astronomical for simple things like checking your email. You could be getting charged for every kilobit that comes in and goes out. Luckily, there are some ways to make sure you don't come home to a bill the size of a mortgage payment. First, you have to decide if you want to be able to make calls while you travel. If so, you may need to contact your carrier and make sure that international calling is enabled on your account. The next thing you want to make sure of is that you aren't roaming on a data network. To prevent this from happening, make sure your **Data Roaming** is set to OFF (tap on the Settings app, tap General, then tap Cellular). Of course, this means that you won't be able to surf the web, check email, etc., while you're out and about. However, you will still be able to connect to Wi-Fi networks. Let's say that you are willing to pay for data roaming, then you can turn Data Roaming on, but I recommend that you turn off Push (on the Settings screen, tap Mail, Contacts, Calendars, then tap **Fetch New Data**), so that your iPhone isn't constantly checking for new email. Also, change the Fetch setting to Manually. This way, you'll only be using data when you manually check for email, or surf the web, or run web-based apps.

Create Your Own Ringtones or Text Tones with GarageBand

You can make your own ringtones or text tones using Apple's GarageBand (4.1.1 or higher), which is included with iLife '11 and ships on all new Macs. To make a custom ringtone or text tone in GarageBand, launch the GarageBand application found in your Applications folder on your Mac, click iPhone Ringtone in the GarageBand new project dialog, then create a new song. Now you can either mix your own track using the software instruments, real instruments (if you're musically inclined), software loops, or vocals from your built-in or external microphone. If you're not musically inclined, you can import one of the many supported sound file formats, such as MP3. Trim your song or composition to be no longer than 40 seconds (2–5 seconds for text tones) and make sure it's set to loop. Once you have built the perfect tone, choose **Send Ringtone to iTunes** from the Share menu. Your custom ringtone or text tone will be created and will be available in your iTunes Tones Library. You can then sync it and use it on your iPhone.

Create Your Own Ringtones or Text Tones with iTunes

You may want to make a ringtone or text tone from a sound file or song in your iTunes Music Library—maybe one of your kids singing or a song from a CD (MP3s and AAC files work great)—but it takes a few steps: First, in your iTunes preferences, make sure before you import the song that your Import Using preference is set to AAC Encoder (choose Preferences from the iTunes [PC: Edit] menu, click the General icon, then click the **Import Settings button**). Listen to your song and find the 30 seconds (or less) of the song that you want (2–5 seconds for text tones) and note the segment start and end times in the progress bar at the top of the iTunes window. Choose Get Info from the File menu, click on the Options tab, enter the Start Time and Stop Time for your 30-second (or less) tone, and click OK. Choose **Create AAC Version** from the Advanced menu and this will create a 30-second version of the song, right beneath the original. Right-click on it and choose **Show in Finder (PC: Show in Windows Explorer)**. When the file appears, duplicate it and change the copy's extension from .m4a to .m4r, and then go back to iTunes and delete the 30-second version you created earlier. Now go back to the Finder window and drag the new .m4r version of your file onto the iTunes icon in your Dock (on a PC, drag it into your Tones Library) to import your new tone into your Tones Library. When you connect your iPhone to iTunes, your new tone will be available in your Tones Library to sync. Don't forget to go back and turn off the Start Time and Stop Time checkboxes for your original song, so that it will play all the way through. Here's a quick video on how to create a tone: **http://bit.ly/createaniPhoneringtone**.

Get a More Accurate Battery Status

On your iPhone, you can turn on a Battery Percentage display. When it's turned on, you'll see the percentage of battery charge next to the battery icon on the right side of the Status Bar at the top of your screen. Go to Settings, tap General, and then tap Usage. Here you can turn **Battery Percentage** on or off.

What to Do with Your Old iPhone

If you're upgrading to a new iPhone, then chances are you probably want to know what to do with your old iPhone. The good news is there are some great options:

Option 1: Pass it down to a family member or friend
Once you upgrade, your old iPhone can be given to someone and they'll just need to take it to a local carrier's store to get a new SIM card (if needed) and have the iPhone activated.

Option 2: Use it as an iPod touch
Since it's already activated, just with no working phone number, you can pull the SIM card out and use it as an iPod and Internet device using Wi-Fi.

Option 3: Sell it
Lastly, if you want to recoup some value out of it, you can sell it. Although the market can be somewhat flooded and there are scammers out there, too, you can fetch a fair price for your older model at places like www.nextworth.com.

Before you pass it on to someone else, though, be sure to wipe your information off of it. Tap on the Settings app, then tap General, and then tap Reset. Then just tap the **Erase All Content and Settings button**.

Send Mail from a Backup Server

If you have more than one email account, then chances are you have multiple SMTP (outgoing) email servers to choose from. Depending on the ISP (Internet service provider), you may be able to set up a backup or secondary email server to send mail from when you're on the go. For example, when I'm at home or on the road, I typically send mail from my Comcast email server. However, if their server is down, then I want to be able to send mail through either my yahoo.com server or my iCloud server. You can set up your backup email server in your iPhone's email settings. First, tap on the Settings app, then tap Mail, Contacts, Calendars. Next, tap the email account that you wish to set up with a backup SMTP server. This brings up the Account screen (you may have to tap Account to get there). Now, scroll down to **SMTP**, and tap it. You'll then get a list of additional servers that you can choose from to make your backup server. Just tap on Off to the right of any SMTP servers that you want as your backup and then tap OFF next to Server at the top to turn it on.

Create a Custom Wallpaper Image

Creating a custom wallpaper image is a good way to have an ICE (In Case of Emergency) contact display on your iPhone (or your name and contact info, in case your iPhone is lost or stolen). Just put the ICE info for your emergency contact, and any other important information (such as medical conditions or allergies), right on your wallpaper image (by creating a custom image on your computer in a program like Photoshop, or taking a photo that includes your ICE or own contact info). Even if your iPhone is secured with a passcode, the information will still be displayed (you can still see part of the wallpaper when your iPhone is locked), so if something happens to you, rescue and medical personnel will know whom to contact.

---

iTip **Use an App to Create an ICE Image**

There is an app called ICE (In Case of Emergency) that is available from the App Store. This app will allow you to build a custom wallpaper image from one of your existing pictures right on your iPhone. It's what I used for the wallpaper you see in the iPhone capture above.

Take a Screenshot

If you want to take a picture (screenshot) of something on your iPhone, there's a way to do it. Just press-and-hold the **Home button** and then press the **Sleep/Wake button** at the top right of the iPhone. The screen will flash white for a second (like a camera flash), and whatever was on your screen at the time will be saved to your Camera Roll as a PNG file. You can then email or text that file to someone, tweet it, post it to Facebook, print it, or sync/download it to your computer the next time you connect your iPhone to it.

Shake to Undo and Shake to Shuffle

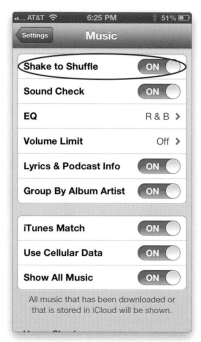

If you type something by accident, there is no Command-Z or Ctrl-Z shortcut to undo it like on your Mac or PC. However, there is a very cool way to undo on your iPhone that reminds me of the Etch A Sketch days—just shake your iPhone and, from the menu that pops up, tap **Undo Typing** to undo what you just typed. Unfortunately, shaking to undo is limited to just typing at this point. If you're listening to your Music app, you can also shake to shuffle to another song. Luckily, if you're a runner, there is a way to turn this feature off in the Music app settings (just tap on the Settings app, then **Music**).

Find Out How Much Data You're Using

If you have AT&T as your service provider, you can keep tabs on your data use to make sure you're not going over what your plan allows. Go to the Phone app, dial *DATA# (*3282#), and tap **Call**. This will trigger a text message to be sent to you, updating you on your data use for your current billing cycle.

Protect Your iPhone

Password Protect It: If your iPhone is ever lost or stolen, the last thing you want to worry about is not only having to replace it, but all the information that someone will now have access to. So, tap on Settings, then on General, then on Passcode Lock. Tap on **Turn Passcode On** and set up a passcode. You'll have to enter the passcode after the time interval that you set (by tapping Require Passcode), but that's a small price to pay for peace of mind.

Buy AppleCare: If you plan on keeping your current iPhone for the length of your service contract (usually two years), then you should consider getting AppleCare. Your original Apple warranty is only for one year, and if it breaks after that, it could be expensive to fix it. AppleCare will cover it for any issues that arise that weren't caused by misuse (for example, dropping it, getting it wet, etc., are not covered).

Set Up iCloud: iCloud is a free online service Apple offers, which includes email, wireless syncing of data, online storage, and other features like Find My iPhone. Find My iPhone can not only locate your iPhone anywhere in the world, but it can also lock and track it, as well as wipe it remotely. See Chapter 7 for more on Find My iPhone.

Back It Up: With all the wireless syncing that you can do, you will be tempted to sync your iPhone less via your computer. You should still connect it and sync regularly. You can also set it to back up to iCloud.

Reading ePubs and PDFs in the iBooks App

You can read ePubs and PDFs in the iBooks app (you can download it for free from the iTunes App Store) either by choosing Open in iBooks in a compatible app, such as Mail, or syncing them directly from iTunes and then opening them in the iBooks app. For example, let's say you receive a PDF attachment in an email. When you tap the attachment to view it, Mail will display it. However, in the upper-right corner, there'll be a button that looks like a box with an arrow coming out of it and when you tap it, you'll see a choice of apps that you have installed that can view PDFs, as well as Mail, Print, and Copy buttons. Tapping **Open in iBooks** will copy the PDF into the iBooks app, where it will appear under PDFs. Now you no longer have to dig up an email just to view the PDFs (or ePubs) you want and this is a great way to carry around your PDF manuals. If you create your own ePub in an application, like Adobe InDesign or Apple's Pages, you can view it directly in iBooks, as well.

Why You Should Encrypt Your iPhone's Backup

iTunes offers the ability to encrypt your iPhone's backup and while you may think that it's overkill, there's a hidden benefit there. If you ever upgrade to a new iPhone or have to replace your existing one, having an encrypted backup to restore from means that iTunes will also restore your passwords in your various apps. Without an encrypted backup, iTunes (Apple) won't take the risk of restoring your iPhone's keychain data as a security precaution. For example, if someone stole your computer, they could restore your data to a different iPhone and have access to all your passwords. If your backup data is encrypted, your passwords are not restored without a password. So, in iTunes, just turn on the **Encrypt iPhone Backup checkbox** on the Summary pane and enter a password for your backup. You'll be a little safer and you'll have the convenience of your new iPhone being all set up with the same information, apps, and passwords that were saved on your old one.

Track Your Package

If you receive a package shipment confirmation email with a link to the tracking information, just tap the link and you'll be taken to Safari to see the tracking information. However, if someone just emails you the tracking number and they don't link to the shipping service's page, your iPhone will automatically detect common tracking numbers and turn them into hyperlinks. Just tap-and-hold on the tracking number in your email, then tap the **Track Shipment button**, and it will automatically take you to the shipper's site to track the package. This won't work for everything, but it works great for UPS tracking numbers, in particular.

Chapter Fourteen
Setting Me Off
The Ins and Outs of Your iPhone's Settings

 I was a bit concerned about using the song title "Setting Me Off" for this chapter, because I thought it might sound too aggressive for a chapter on something as non-confrontational as learning about which iPhone settings do what. But then when I learned (by doing a quick search in the iTunes Store) that the group that recorded the song was named Speed\Kill/Hate (from their album *Acts of Insanity*), I felt much better about it. Well, that was until I noticed that the iTunes Store people had added an Explicit label beside the song's name (they do this as a warning to parents because, frankly, kids couldn't care less. In fact, I imagine that when a teen sees an Explicit label beside a song, to them it means "This is for you!"). Anyway, once I saw that label, I did what any responsible adult would do—I double-clicked on it to hear the free 90-second preview. It was a heavy metal song and, I have to be honest with you, I must be getting really old, because I couldn't understand a single word he sang. He could have been reading a *Sopranos* script set to music, containing every four-letter word known to merchant marines, and there is no possible way I would have been able to discern even one. Luckily, my son has a special CD player (generally used only by DJs) that lets you slow the speed of the CD down, and it was only then that I was able to hear the lyrics for the opening verse of "Setting Me Off," which were: "Don't go changin'...to try and please me. You never let me down before...oooh, oooh, oooh...oooh, oooooh." So, I felt pretty good about it.

Using Your iPhone on an Airplane

Most airlines won't let you have your iPhone (or any other device that transmits) on during takeoff and landing. But, you'll probably want to do other stuff with it while in the air, so Apple included Airplane mode. While in this mode, the phone, Wi-Fi, Bluetooth transceivers, and GPS reception are turned off. To switch to Airplane mode, tap on the Settings app, and then tap on the word OFF next to **Airplane Mode** at the top to turn it on. You'll know you're in Airplane mode because there will be a little airplane icon in the upper-left corner where your carrier's logo used to be. Once you land, you can turn Airplane mode back off by tapping on the Airplane Mode ON button in the Settings screen.

---

iTip **Other Reasons to Use Airplane Mode**

Although Airplane mode was designed for use on airplanes, it's also useful in other situations, such as being near a P.A. system mic, or during a recording session, or being near your stereo speakers, where there may be interference from your GSM-based iPhone. If you start to hear a loud buzzing sound coming from these other sources, it may be your iPhone causing it. Go into Airplane mode to stop it.

Connecting to Wi-Fi

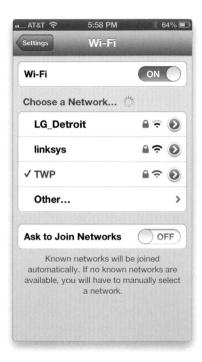

Tap on the Settings app, then tap on Wi-Fi, and turn **Wi-Fi** off or on by tapping on the ON/OFF button. You'll see the available networks that your iPhone sees and may be connected to. If there is a little Lock icon next to the network name, then that network is locked with a password (the iPhone supports both WEP and WPA security). So, if you know the password, you can type it in and log on. If there is a network that you're near that isn't broadcasting its name (it's cloaked), you can tap Other, type in the network name, and choose the type of security the network is using so that you can type in the appropriate password or HEX key. Lastly, there is an Ask to Join Networks option, and it's important to know about this one, because while you're out and about, there may be lots of Wi-Fi networks in the area. When you go to use the data features of your iPhone, if it sees an open Wi-Fi network, your iPhone will ask you to join it rather than using your carrier's 4G, 3G, or EDGE network. If you find this constant asking annoying, you can turn this off. However, then it will be up to you to check to see if there is a network available.

---

iTip   **On a Flight with Wi-Fi Access?**

If you're on a flight that offers Wi-Fi, you can turn it back on after you've placed your iPhone in Airplane mode for takeoff and landing. Just go to the Settings app, tap Wi-Fi, then tap the available Wi-Fi network to turn it back on and connect to the in-flight wireless. Your iPhone will stay in Airplane mode, and your Phone features will still be off.

Using Virtual Private Networks (VPN)

The average iPhone user will never connect to a VPN. This is a feature primarily used by companies and people that wish to access office/home network services remotely. If your company supports VPN, then chat with your IT staff to get the settings for your iPhone to be able to connect to your Virtual Private Network. Once configured (in the General settings, tap on **VPN**), just tap the VPN OFF button (which will now appear on the Settings screen) to turn it on and connect. Then, once connected, you can use your Safari browser and perhaps specific corporate apps to access your company's internal services and websites.

Don't Want to Be Disturbed?

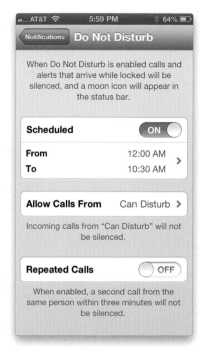

iOS 6 includes a new Do Not Disturb mode, which is great for people who want to keep their iPhone on, but don't want to be disturbed by alert sounds and phone calls. Unlike the Ring/Silent switch, when your iPhone is in Do Not Disturb mode, it won't vibrate, make any sounds of any kind, or light the Lock screen when you receive notifications. Do Not Disturb is one of my favorite new features, because as a frequent international traveler, I'm often in different time zones and want to keep my iPhone on for emergencies, but don't want to receive calls that can wait. To turn on Do Not Disturb, tap on the Settings app, then just tap on the **Do Not Disturb OFF button** to turn it on. You can enable several Do Not Disturb options, as well, by tapping Notifications (right below it in the Settings app) and then tapping **Do Not Disturb**. Here, you can set a schedule that will automatically enable and disable Do Not Disturb each day (although you can set exceptions). Tap the Scheduled ON/OFF button to turn it on, and then set the From and To times to your desired times. You can also choose a group of contacts that are allowed to ring your iPhone when it's in Do Not Disturb mode by tapping on Allow Calls From. Lastly, if you turn on Repeated Calls, this will allow someone's call to come through if they call, hang up, and call you back within three minutes. By the way, when Do Not Disturb is turned on, you'll see a little crescent moon icon at the top of your screen.

Manage Your Push Notifications

Your iPhone has a Notification Center, where an app sends you a notification without it actually having to be running in the foreground. For example, the CNN app can pop up a message when there is a breaking news story; the Facebook app can alert you when someone just tagged you in a photo; the Google Voice app can let you know that you just received a message; etc. You can choose to get a Sound, a Badge, a Banner, an Alert, or any combination of those, or turn it off altogether. You can control how each app notifies you in the Notification settings, including whether or not it appears on the Lock screen (tap on the Settings app, then tap on **Notifications**). For example, if someone posts a message on my Facebook wall, it's not an emergency—it can wait. I don't want to see a Banner or Alert every time that happens. If I leave Badge App Icon on, then I'll just get a numeric badge over the Facebook app icon on my Home screen, letting me know how many alerts I've missed. In most cases, you can turn on/off each type of notification for each app. To get to the Notification Center and see all your notifications, just swipe down from the top of any screen.

---

iTip See Weather Forecast

If you have the Weather displaying at the top of your Notification Center, you can swipe to the left or right to see the forecast.

Your iPhone's General Settings

In the General settings screen in the Settings app, tapping **About** gives you almost all the information you could need about your iPhone. You'll find things like the number of songs, videos, and photos that you have, as well as the amount of available space, serial number of your iPhone, software version, and firmware version. You'll also find the MAC addresses for Wi-Fi and Bluetooth chips. In the **Keyboard** screen, you'll be able to turn on/off the Enable Caps Lock function, as well as the other auto Keyboard features. You can even set up a four-digit password that would have to be typed in to unlock your iPhone in the **Passcode Lock** screen. For those needing to set up a VPN (Virtual Private Network) connection to access their corporate network, you would do that on the **VPN** screen (you'll need the VPN settings from your company's IT department). Lastly, if you have a teenager with an iPhone, you can set up some restrictions here by tapping **Restrictions**. (*Note:* We'll look at some of the other General settings throughout this chapter.)

Updating Your Software Over the Air

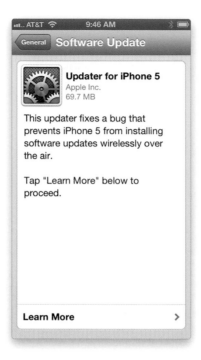

When it comes time to update your iPhone's operating system (iOS), you can do it over the air. This means that when Apple updates the iOS, you don't have to plug in your iPhone to your computer to update it. The updates are now smaller, so you can even do many of them via a cellular network. To check to see if you have a Software Update pending, just tap General in the Settings app, and then tap **Software Update**.

Checking Your iPhone Usage

The Usage screen gives you a quick look at your iPhone usage (tap on the Settings app, then tap on General, and then tap on **Usage**). At the top of the Usage screen, you will see how much space your apps are taking up. You will also see how much space is being taken up in your iCloud account. You have the option of seeing the percentage of battery life left next to the battery icon at the top right of your screen. The Usage screen also lists the number of hours and minutes of usage and standby since your last full charge. This is great for tracking battery life. If you tap the Cellular Usage button, it will also show you your call time and your cellular network data usage. If you want to start tracking these statistics from scratch, just tap the Reset Statistics button to start them over again at zero. Your Current Period call time and Cellular Network Data statistics will be reset, but your Lifetime call time and battery usage will not be.

Understanding Your Cellular Settings

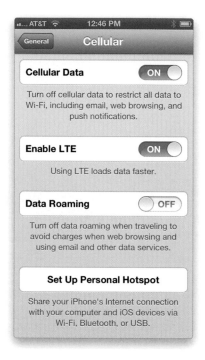

When you tap **Cellular**, on the General settings screen in the Settings app, you can see and control how your iPhone uses your carrier's data network. The first option is to turn Cellular Data on or off. I can't imagine, though, too many times where you'd turn this off. One instance that comes to mind is if you have a really limited data plan and you want to make sure that your iPhone doesn't accidently use cellular data while you're on Wi-Fi, then you'd turn Cellular Data off. If you have an iPhone 5, you can turn LTE (4G) on or off. If you're not in an area covered by your provider's LTE coverage, then you definitely want to turn Enable LTE off to save battery life. Data Roaming should almost always be off. This will prevent your iPhone from using very expensive data roaming when you travel abroad. It is off by default, and should only be turned on if you knowingly paid for international data roaming ahead of time. If you scroll down, you'll see options to turn cellular data on or off for specific iOS features, such as iCloud Documents, FaceTime, etc. Turning these off will save you from using unnecessary data on a limited data plan.

Using Your iPhone to Connect Your Laptop or Other Wi-Fi Device to the Internet

This is called a Personal Hotspot, and it allows you to use your iPhone's 4G or 3G data connection to provide Internet access to your laptop (or other Wi-Fi-enabled device). You can connect to your iPhone via Wi-Fi, Bluetooth, or USB (using your sync cable). In order for you to use a Personal Hotspot, your carrier must support it, and they may charge you an additional monthly fee to use it. To enable a Personal Hotspot on your account, tap on the Settings app, then tap on General. Tap on Cellular, then tap on **Set Up Personal Hotspot**. Once it's enabled, just turn it on and connect your iPhone to your laptop. Once you're connected, a blue band will appear at the top of the iPhone screen (as seen on the right above). If your laptop has Wi-Fi or Bluetooth, then this will let you connect to the Internet from wherever you have 4G or 3G data coverage without even having to take your iPhone out of your pocket or purse. Bluetooth is rated for distances up to 30 feet. *Note:* AT&T has Personal Hotspot support for the iPhone. However, you'll have to make a choice: if you're currently grandfathered in from a previous iPhone and have an unlimited data plan, you cannot sign up for this without giving up that unlimited plan.

Sync Your iPhone Over Wi-Fi

Before iOS 5, you always had to plug in your USB cable to your Mac or PC to sync new media and to back up your iPhone. Now, you only need to plug it in one more time, just long enough to enable Wi-Fi Sync. In the Summary tab of iTunes, under Options, turn on the **Sync with This iPhone Over Wi-Fi checkbox**. Once you enable it, you can disconnect your iPhone (let the current sync finish first) and, from that point on, whenever you connect your iPhone to a power source, it will begin syncing with your computer via Wi-Fi. You will need to have iTunes running on your computer for Wi-Fi Sync to work. You can also initiate a wireless sync whenever you want by going into the Settings app, tapping on General, tapping on iTunes Wi-Fi Sync, and then just tapping the **Sync Now button**. It even works with more than one computer, keeping in mind that you can only sync one category (Data, Media, Photos, Apps, etc.) to one computer at a time. In my case, I sync media (music, movies, tones, books, podcasts) from my iMac and everything else from my MacBook Pro.

Control Your Spotlight Searches

You can control your search results better when using the global Spotlight search feature. Tap on the Settings app, then General, and then tap on **Spotlight Search**. Here, you can not only check and uncheck the categories you want searched, but more importantly, you can reorder them in the priority that you want the results to show (by just tapping on the three bars to the right of any search option and dragging it where you want it). For example, I rarely use this feature to search for music (or other Music app or Videos app items), and I don't want those results to show first, so I moved Music, Podcasts, Videos, and Audiobooks lower in the list (if I'm searching for "Scott," I'm probably looking for a contact named Scott and not Jill Scott. :)

Don't Forget to Set Your Time Zone

If you travel to different time zones, you'll have to decide how you want your iPhone to handle the times for events in your calendar. For example, let's say you have an appointment set for 12:00 p.m. Eastern time. When you go to California, which is on Pacific time, do you want the event to display as 12:00 p.m. or 9:00 a.m.? If you leave Time Zone Support off, then the event will automatically adjust based upon the time zone you're in. So, your appointment would display as 9:00 a.m. If you want it to display the time you set the appointment for, no matter what time zone you're in, then you would turn Time Zone Support on and set your home/default time zone. Tap on the Settings app and then tap Mail, Contacts, Calendars. Scroll down to the Calendars section and tap **Time Zone Support**. By default, Time Zone Support is off (if you wanted to turn it on, tap on OFF). Tap Time Zone and type in your home/default city. If you live in a smaller town, it may not be in the list, so you may have to choose the largest city in your time zone instead. In case you were wondering, I prefer this setting to be off—I want the appointment to be in the local time wherever I am.

Setting Up Your Keyboard

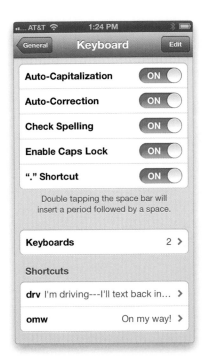

Your onscreen keyboard is the key to using your iPhone successfully, and there are several settings you can use to get it to work just the way you want it to. Tap on General and then tap **Keyboard** in the Settings app. In the Keyboard screen, you have Auto-Capitalization, Auto-Correction, and Check Spelling on by default. Enable Caps Lock is also on, by default. With this on, if you double-tap the Shift key on your keyboard, Caps Lock will be enabled. Also with the "." Shortcut option on, when you double-tap the Spacebar on your keyboard after a sentence, it will place a period and a space, and capitalize the next word. The Keyboard screen is also where you can enable additional keyboards, such as the popular Emoji keyboard to use those cool emoticons (see Chapter 13 for more on these). Lastly, there's a Shortcuts feature, which is awesome. You can create shortcuts that can type lots of words for you with just a few characters. For example, you can create a shortcut like "drv" that enters "I'm driving right now and can't text" (see Chapter 3 for more on these).

Choosing Your Primary Language

In the International settings (in the General settings of the Settings app, tap on **International**), you can choose your primary language, as well as formats for your Calendar. You can also choose your language for Voice Control and turn on international keyboards, if needed.

Settings for the Visually, Hearing, Learning, and Physically Impaired

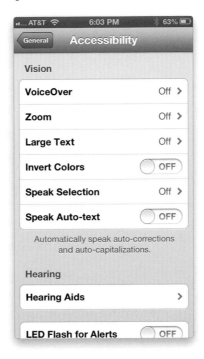

iOS 6 has a slew of Accessibility settings for the visually, hearing, learning, and physically impaired. Just tap **Accessibility** in the General settings of the Settings app. There, you will be able to turn on features for Vision, Hearing, Learning, and Physical & Motor. Each of these options can be turned on or off at any time to make it easier to hear, see, and use your iPhone.

Choosing and Managing Sounds

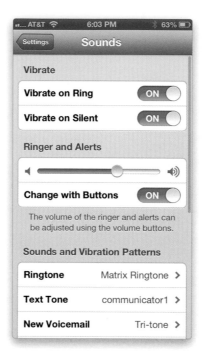

The Sounds screen (tap on the Settings app, then tap on **Sounds**) controls all the alert sounds your iPhone makes. You can turn your Vibrate settings on or off (by default, Vibrate is on for both the Silent and Ring modes. So even if you use the external Ring/Silent switch to turn the ringer on or off, the phone will vibrate when you receive a call). You can change the Vibrate settings for both Silent and Ring independently of each other. You can also change your Ring volume here by dragging the little knob (circle) on the slider with the speakers on both ends, and choose a default ringtone. The iPhone's default ringtone is Marimba, however, you can pick from a list of 25 different ringtones, and any custom ringtones you've added, by tapping Ringtone. The ringtone you pick is how the iPhone will ring for all incoming calls, except those of contacts that you've assigned custom ringtones to. You also have the ability to set custom Text Tones. You can buy new ones in the iTunes app or make your own on your computer (see Chapter 13 for more on making your own). The iPhone makes sounds every time you receive a new text message, voicemail message, email, tweet, Facebook post, calendar alarm, or Reminder alert. It also makes sounds when you send email, tap on the keyboard, or when the iPhone locks. You can turn these sounds on or off individually for each area.

Adjusting the Brightness and Changing Your Wallpaper

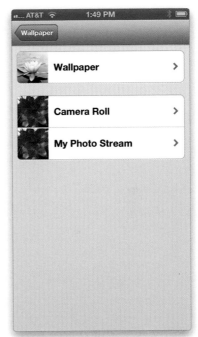

The iPhone screen is very bright, and it automatically adjusts under certain conditions to conserve battery life. But, if you want to manually adjust the brightness, you can. Tap the **Brightness & Wallpaper button** in the Settings screen and drag the slider to the left to make the screen dimmer or to the right to make it brighter. You can also turn off Auto-Brightness if you like by tapping on the ON/OFF button. Also in the Brightness & Wallpaper screen are your wallpaper options. When you first turn on your iPhone or wake it from sleep, it displays a photo of rippling water. But, if you want to choose a different picture, tap the **Wallpaper button**. You'll have a choice between the Apple-supplied wallpaper photos in the Wallpaper screen or your own photos that you either took with your iPhone camera or synced from your computer. Find the photo you want to use as your wallpaper and tap on it. You'll be able to resize it using two fingers and move it around. Once it looks the way you want, tap the Set button. You'll also have the choice of setting it for your Lock Screen, Home Screen, or both. This means that you can have two different wallpaper images: one for your Lock screen and one as the background for your Home screens.

Controlling Your Privacy Settings

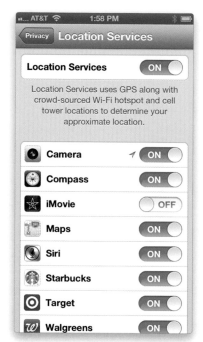

There are lots of apps out there that can take advantage of your Location Services information. You can control whether or not an app has access to your location on an app-by-app basis. For example, perhaps you want to be able to find the closest restaurant, but you don't want the pictures you take at your private home to be geotagged. No problem, just tap on the Settings app, tap on Privacy, then tap on **Location Services**, and turn on or off the ones you want to know or not know your location. If you see a little arrow next to the ON/OFF button of one of your apps, it means that particular app is using Location Services right now. You can also control which apps have access to your Contacts, Calendars, Reminders, Photos, Bluetooth Sharing, Twitter, and Facebook settings in the Privacy screen.

---

iTip **Turn Off Location Services to Save Battery Life**

Location Services is great, however it does drain your battery faster. So, if you're not currently using any location-aware apps, then go ahead and turn off Location Services (at the top of the Location Services settings screen) to save power.

Setting Up Your Mail, Contacts, and Calendar Apps

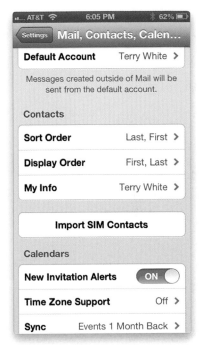

In the Mail, Contacts, Calendars screen in the Settings app, you can see, change, or add email accounts. However, you can also change the settings for the way the iPhone works with your existing email accounts, contacts, and calendars. By default, the iPhone shows you the 50 most recent messages, which you can change to 100, 200, 500, or 1,000. It also shows you the first two lines of the incoming message without having to open the message, which you can change from zero to five lines. You can turn on Show To/Cc Label of your incoming messages, which will put a little To or CC in front of your name to let you know if the message was sent to you or you were just copied on it. When you delete a message on your iPhone, it does it immediately. However, if you'd like a warning, you can turn on Ask Before Deleting. You can have images received in emails load manually or automatically by turning Load Remote Images on or off. Turning on Organize By Thread keeps all replies from a single email together, as if in a subfolder for that email message. If you want to have Mail always blind copy you on your outgoing messages, you can turn on Always Bcc Myself. With Increase Quote Level turned on, an indent is added when you reply or forward a message. The iPhone puts a cool "Sent from my iPhone"message at the end of every email that you send out and you can edit this by tapping Signature (in iOS 6, you can now create different signatures for each email account). You can also choose how your contacts are displayed and sorted. If you're upgrading from a different kind of phone that stores the contacts on the SIM card, you can import those contacts. This is the screen that also lets you set options for your calendar and reminder alerts, and decide how far back to sync events that have passed.

Setting Up Your Notes App

The Notes app is pretty handy for jotting down notes on the go. If you have an iPhone 5 or 4S, you can even dictate them. You can change the default font to one that's easier for you to read (in the Settings app, tap on **Notes**), and more importantly, if you have more than one email account that supports Notes, you can choose a default email account to sync your Notes with. This is handy when you want to create notes in one place (say your computer) and read them in another place (say your iPhone). *Note:* This may not be available on all carriers.

Setting Up Your Phone App

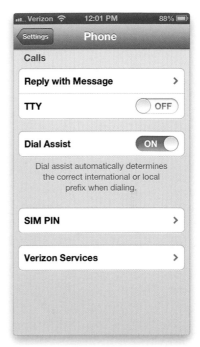

In the Phone settings, within the Calls section, you can change the message that is sent when you tap the Reply with Message button (the little phone icon that appears on the bottom right of the screen when you get a call). You can also enable Call Forwarding to have your incoming calls automatically forwarded to another number. Call Waiting can be turned off, so that if you're on a call and another call comes in, it will be sent to voice-mail immediately. You can also turn off the Show My Caller ID feature. However, keep in mind that many people don't accept calls from numbers that are blocked. (*Note:* These options are for AT&T service, and may vary if you have a different service provider—see Verizon's options above right.) For the hearing impaired, you can turn on the TTY (Tele-typewriter) feature, and Apple does sell an iPhone TTY adapter separately that allows you to connect your iPhone to teletype machines. Depending on your service provider, you may be able to change your voicemail password here, as well. Next is a feature called Dial Assist that will automatically add the appropriate prefix numbers to your calls back home when you're traveling abroad or making calls locally. The last two options are SIM PIN and Services for your provider. Enabling a SIM PIN makes it harder for someone to take your SIM card and use it in another phone. If your provider uses the Services option, you'll be able to access things like speed dial numbers to check your bill balance and directory assistance.

Setting Up Your Messages App

Your Messages app allows you to send/receive SMS/MMS messages to/from other phones. However, it also supports Apple's iMessage. When iMessage is on (it is by default and is found on the **Messages** settings screen), your Messages app will automatically detect if you're sending a text or picture message to another iOS 5 or later user, or a Mac user running OS X 10.8 Mountain Lion or later, and send it via iMessage instead of your cellular carrier's SMS system. The main benefit here is that iMessages don't count against your SMS/text message plan, especially if you're on a limited one. You can turn on Send Read Receipts, so that others will know when you've read their message. The next option is Send as SMS. This is on by default and will send your message as a regular SMS/MMS to a user when iMessage fails. Tap on Send & Receive to add your email address(es) that you want to be able to receive iMessages at, too. This way, a user can send you an iMessage without having to know your phone number. With Group Messaging on (by default, near the bottom), when you send a message to a group of people and they reply, the reply will go to everyone in the group.

Setting Up FaceTime

FaceTime allows you to do video chats with any other iPhone 5, 4S, or 4, iPad with Retina display, iPad 2, iPad mini, iPod touch, or Mac user. FaceTime works via Wi-Fi, so there is no additional cost and it doesn't chew up your data plan. By default, your iPhone uses your phone number to receive FaceTime requests. On other devices, such as an iPad or Mac, you can use either an email address or iPhone phone number (provided the Mac is running Mac OS X 10.8 Mountain Lion or later and the iOS device is running iOS 5 or later). You can add your email addresses to your FaceTime settings on your iPhone, too. This way, if an iPad, Mac, or iPod touch user attempts to FaceTime you via your email address, you'll still get the notification. Just tap on the Settings app, then scroll down and tap on **FaceTime**. You can use your Apple ID or tap on Add An Email and add as many of your email addresses as you want. Also new in iOS 6, you can now use FaceTime over your carrier's cellular network provided that you have a plan that supports this (just tap the Use Cellular Data OFF button to turn it on). This means that you can use Face-Time when you're out and about and not necessarily on Wi-Fi. *Note:* Using FaceTime via cellular will definitely impact the data on your data plan, though.

Setting Up Your Maps App

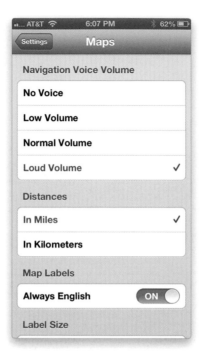

In iOS 6, Apple introduced the Apple Maps app to replace the Google Maps app. With this addition, there is now a Maps settings screen in the Settings app. In the Maps settings, you can control the Navigation Voice Volume, whether your Distances are in miles or kilometers, whether your Map Labels always use your default language, and the Label Size.

Setting Up Your Safari Web Browser

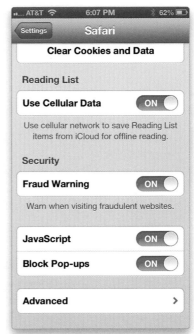

Using the Safari settings screen, you can change your default search engine—whether you prefer Google search, Yahoo search, or Bing search, you can change that here. There is a Fraud Warning setting (by default, it's on). This will help warn you if you visit a site that is known to be compromised by malicious code. By default, the iPhone also has JavaScript and Block Pop-Ups on. You can turn each of these off if you need to. Safari is set to accept cookies from visited sites. Other than Never, this is probably the safest setting. Cookies are good in the fact that they minimize the need on many sites to have to constantly log in. Your login info or site settings can be stored as a cookie right in your iPhone's Safari browser. In this screen, you can also choose to clear your browsing history, and Clear Cookies and Data to remove any trace of your having been to the sites you've been to. You can also turn on the AutoFill setting near the top of the Safari screen, so that when you visit sites that require you to type in passwords or other information, such as your address, you can just tap the AutoFill button to have those pieces of info automatically filled in.

Setting Up Your iTunes and App Store Apps

If you tap on the Settings app, then tap on **iTunes & App Stores**, you can turn on iTunes Match if you subscribe to this service from Apple. You can also turn on Automatic Downloads for Music, Apps, or Books, so that any of those you purchase on your computer or other iDevice will be automatically downloaded to your iPhone. The next option is to turn on or off cellular data for your downloads. If you have a limited data plan, you may want to turn this off so that your iTunes downloads only happen when you're connected to Wi-Fi. If you have any apps that can automatically download content, such as newspaper or magazine apps, you'll be able to control them individually here. At the top, you'll see your Apple ID. You can tap it to sign out or switch user accounts.

Setting Up Your Music App

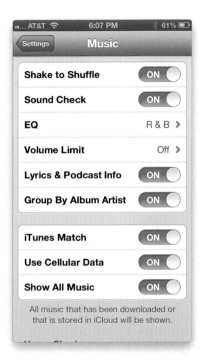

There are some cool settings for the Music app (found in the Settings app, under **Music**): The first one allows you to shake your iPhone to shuffle your songs. Next is Sound Check, and with this on, your iPhone's Music app attempts to balance the sound levels of your songs. So, for example, if you have one song that is really loud and another song that isn't so loud, with Sound Check on, it should lower the volume of the really loud song and raise the volume of the song that isn't so loud. The next setting is for EQ (equalizer). It's possible (and recommended) to set the EQ setting for each of your songs in iTunes on your computer. You can set all your rock tracks to the Rock EQ setting, all your R&B to the R&B EQ setting, all your jazz to the Jazz EQ setting, etc. When they are played on your iPhone, they'll sound better. But, you can also set a default EQ setting on your iPhone for the songs that don't have an EQ setting. You can only pick one, so pick the one that would cover most of your music collection. Next, you can set a volume limit. This will limit the volume across the board. With Lyrics & Podcast Info on, you can tap a song's album artwork to see its lyrics, if you've added them in iTunes on your computer, or tap on a podcast you're playing to get information about what's in that podcast. iTunes Match is an optional paid service ($24.99/year) that allows you to have all of your music synced to iCloud and streamed to your iPhone. At the bottom is the Home Sharing section, which gives you access to your music from your computer running iTunes over your Wi-Fi network.

Setting Up Your Videos App

The Videos app is where you go to play any video content stored on your iPhone, such as movies, TV shows, video podcasts, and music videos. The Videos settings are pretty straight-forward. The first setting is to play videos from where you left off as opposed to starting from the beginning each time, and the second one is to turn on Closed Captioning or not, if the video has closed captioning in it. You also have a Home Sharing section, which allows you to stream videos from your computer running iTunes over your Wi-Fi network.

Setting Up Your Photos and Camera Apps

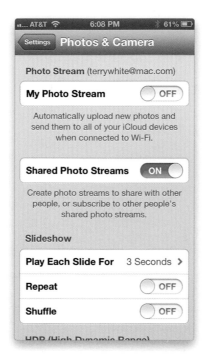

There are six basic settings for the Photos and Camera apps (in the Settings app, tap on **Photos & Camera**). The first setting is for Photo Stream. Photo Stream is part of Apple's free iCloud service (for more on iCloud, see Chapter 9). With Photo Stream on, the photos you take with your iPhone will automatically be synced to iCloud and then made available on your other devices that have Photo Stream, such as an Apple TV, an iPad, or a Mac running iPhoto. It syncs your 1,000 most recent photos or anything less than 30 days old. In iOS 6, you can also turn on Shared Photo Streams. This allows you to create Photo Streams in the Photos app that you can share with specific individuals and add specific pictures to. The next setting lets you set the duration for each photo during your slide shows. The default is 3 seconds, but you can set it from 2 to 20 seconds. The fourth setting is Repeat. By default, this is off, which means that your slide show will stop after the last slide. You can turn on Repeat so that it loops the slide show. The next setting is Shuffle, which is off by default. With Shuffle on, your slides will play in a random order. Lastly, your iPhone 5, 4S, or 4 can create HDR (High Dynamic Range) photos. This setting lets you keep both the HDR and regular photo, or not.

Setting Up Twitter Integration on Your iPhone

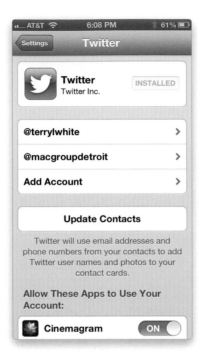

iOS 5 and later include built-in Twitter support. This means that you can send tweets from various apps. For example, if you just took a photo with your iPhone camera, you can actually tweet it right from the Photos app without having to launch the Twitter app first. You can tweet a webpage that you're looking at in the Safari app just by tapping the Share button at the bottom of the Safari screen. However, before you can do any tweeting, you'll need to add your Twitter account to the Twitter settings. Just tap on the Settings app, and then tap **Twitter**. You can add your account and even add multiple accounts. Since the Contacts app has a Twitter field, you can even tap the Update Contacts button to have the settings automatically match up your contacts' email addresses and phone numbers with their Twitter usernames, and then add their Twitter usernames and photos to their contact info on your iPhone. Although iOS integrates with Twitter, it's still a good idea to download the free Twitter app from the App Store (just click the Install button that appears at the top of the Twitter settings screen).

---

iTip Tweet via Siri

You can dictate a tweet to Siri and she'll send it for you. Simply press-and-hold the Home button to bring up Siri and say "Tweet (and whatever it is you want to tweet)." You can even include hash tags by saying "hash tag" and what the tag is at the end of your tweet.

Setting Up Facebook Integration on Your iPhone

In iOS 6 or later, you now have direct support for Facebook just like you do for Twitter. This means that you can post Facebook status updates and pictures directly from apps like Safari, Photos, and even the Notification Center. An added benefit is that you can also have your Facebook friends show up in your Contacts app and have their birthdays show up on your calendar. While these last two features can be helpful, if you have lots of Facebook friends, you may want to turn them off (my calendar became overwhelmed with hundreds of birthdays). To get started, just go to the Settings app, scroll down, and tap on **Facebook**. From there, you can enter your Facebook login information. Then, once signed in, you can turn on/off support for Contacts and Calendar, as well as choose your settings. Lastly, there is an Update All Contacts button. I like this feature because it temporarily grants Facebook access to your existing contacts list, so that it can update your contacts with profile pictures and Facebook profile links. This means that when you go to your Contacts app, you'll see pictures for contacts that you didn't already have pictures for, as well as being able to tap to go right to a particular contact's Facebook page.

Apple ID

scottkelby@mymail.com

View Apple ID

Sign Out

iForgot

Cancel

Chapter Fifteen
The Trouble with Boys
Troubleshooting Your iPhone

 Terry asked me to write this chapter intro for two reasons: (1) it's my job to write the chapter intros, and (2) I'm not really qualified to write anything in a troubleshooting chapter. It's only because nothing has gone the slightest bit wrong with my iPhone since I bought it, so I've never had an occasion to trouble-shoot a problem. On the other hand, Terry (being a renown gadget guru and committed iPhone freak) is very hard on technology. It's not unusual to stop at Terry's house and find him taking some new gadget (like an iPhone) and exposing it to harsher conditions than your average user is likely to experience (unless he or she were to lead an expedition to Antarctica, or do so many bad things that they wind up in "the really hot place" where really bad people go—you know where I'm talking about: Phoenix). Anyway, Terry asked me to write this intro, and I have to tell you, I'm honored to do it. In fact, I'm honored to be sharing the pages of this book with him, because even though many people don't know this, Terry is the reigning Midwest freestyle clogging champion (in the men's 35–45 age bracket), and he competes nationwide at clogging conventions, state fairs, and competitions, including Clogapalooza 2012 where he took third place in the men's individual freestyle competition. I was there cheering Terry on, and I've got to tell you—he was robbed. One of the judges worked for Microsoft and, not coincidentally, was the only one to score Terry's performance as an 8.2 (all the other judges scored him as a 10). What a shame—we really thought it was "his year."

Dropped Calls and Bad Reception

Depending on your carrier and physical location, you may just be in a bad reception area. But, if you feel that it's happening more often than it should, here are some things to remember: Your iPhone has antennas along its sides. Many are saying that physical contact (i.e., your hand) covering the little black strips on the sides will lower your reception. If you're having issues, you may want to invest in a case/cover to help reduce this issue. Also, make sure that you've got the latest software update for your iPhone (go to your Settings app and, under General, tap on **Software Update**). Another thing to try is resetting your Network settings (under General settings, under Reset at the bottom, tap on **Reset Network Settings**). Some find this instantly fixes their problems. Please note that when you do this, it will also blow away any saved Wi-Fi passwords.

---

iTip **Getting Better Reception**

*Simply try turning 3G or 4G (only on an iPhone 5) off. I know that it may sound like a really bad thing, but if you're not actively surfing the web or checking email, then having 3G or 4G on is not really helping you. So try turning it off to see if that improves your reception in troubled areas by tapping on the Settings app, then tapping General, and then tapping Cellular. Tap the **Cellular Data ON/OFF button** to turn it off.*

The Quick Fix for Most Problems

Most problems can be fixed by simply turning your iPhone off and back on again. To turn it off and back on, hold down the **Sleep/Wake button** on the top. After a few seconds, you will get a message that says Slide to Power Off. Go ahead and tap-and-hold on the red arrow button, then slide your finger across to the right to power it off. Once it powers off, you can power it back on by holding down the Sleep/Wake button, again. Once your iPhone comes back on, you can try to do whatever it was that wasn't working before.

Your iPhone Doesn't Come On or Respond

Make sure that your battery is charged—try either connecting it to your computer's USB port or to the AC adapter with the USB cable that came with your iPhone. Its screen should come on when it's connected to a power source and indicate that the battery is charging. If not, then you may want to try rebooting it. Press-and-hold the **Home button** and the **Sleep/Wake button** located on the top of the iPhone until you see the Apple logo. You can let go then and should be back in business. If your iPhone is on but not responding to your touch, you can also try rebooting it the same way. Your iPhone should boot up normally and return to normal operation.

---

iTip Use the USB Cable That Came with Your iPhone

Make sure you use the USB cable that came with your iPhone 5, 4S, or 4, as older cables and chargers may not be compatible. This especially goes for an iPhone 5, since it has a Lightning connector, while the 4 and 4S have a 30-pin connector.

No Sound

There could be several reasons why your iPhone isn't making any sounds. The first thing to check is that you don't have it on Silent, so check the **Ring/Silent switch** on the left side of the iPhone and make sure it's pushed toward the front of the iPhone. If you see an orange bar on the switch, that means that it's on Silent. The next thing to check is the volume. Press the **Volume Up button** on the left side of the iPhone below the Ring/Silent switch (the Ring/Silent switch and the Volume Up and Down buttons are shown circled above). If you're still not hearing anything, then check to make sure the volume is turned up in your app, as well. Make sure there isn't anything plugged into the headset jack, or if you are using headphones, that they are pressed all the way in. Also, make sure that your iPhone isn't in Do Not Disturb mode by going to your Settings app and making sure Do Not Disturb is off. Finally, if you have your iPhone docked in an iPod or iPhone speaker system, make sure that the speaker system has power and is on.

You're on Wi-Fi, but Your iPhone Uses 3G/4G

First, make sure your password has been entered correctly by tapping the Settings app, then tapping Wi-Fi. Tap the blue arrow button next to the name of your network and then tap **Forget This Network**. Try accessing your Wi-Fi network again and re-entering the password. If the WEP password doesn't work, try entering the HEX key. If your router uses MAC address filtering, then you'll need to log onto your router's admin page and enter the iPhone's Wi-Fi address, which can be found on the **About** screen under General settings.

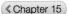

You're on Wi-Fi, but Your iPhone Won't Surf the Web

Some Wi-Fi networks require that you first log in or accept the terms/conditions of their service. This could prevent your apps from getting online, even though it appears that you have a Wi-Fi connection. Another instance would be when you first get on a plane that has Gogo Wi-Fi, which you've used in the past. Your iPhone will automatically connect to the network, but you won't be able to surf because Gogo is disabled while on the ground. In these cases, the easiest thing to do is to bring up your Safari web browser and then try to connect to a webpage. This will either present the page that you need to register/accept the terms on or show you a status of the site. If this still doesn't work, you might try turning off Wi-Fi (in the Settings app) and using your 3G/4G cellular data instead.

You're in a Wi-Fi Hotspot, but Can't Surf the Web

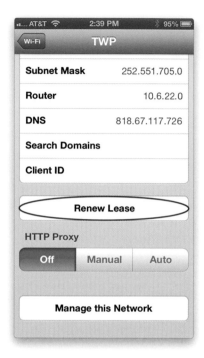

If you're connected to a commercial Wi-Fi hotspot, say at a favorite coffee shop or restaurant, and you're having problems getting onto the Internet, try renewing your DHCP lease. Tap on the Settings app and then tap Wi-Fi. Next, tap the blue arrow button for the network that you're connected to, scroll down, and tap the **Renew Lease button**. This will tell the iPhone to grab an updated IP address, and possibly updated DNS info.

Get a Fresh Start with Your Information

If you want to wipe the Contacts, Calendars, Bookmarks, Notes, or Mail Accounts settings from your iPhone and replace them with what's currently on your computer, you can do this in iTunes. After you connect your iPhone to your computer, click on the Info preferences tab after you click on your iPhone in the Devices list. In the Advanced section, there is a checkbox for each of the items just mentioned that you can turn on to have iTunes overwrite what's currently on the iPhone with what's on your computer. This will be a one-time thing and your iPhone will sync normally the next time you connect it.

---

iTip | **Replace Your Data from iCloud**

I no longer sync my data directly to my computer. Instead, I sync wirelessly via iCloud, so the above tip is not as useful as it used to be. You can go to your iCloud settings on your iPhone and turn off, then back on your Contacts, Calendars, Reminders, etc., to wipe them off your iPhone and download a fresh set when you turn them back on. Or you can use the tip above, if you prefer.

Starting from Scratch

If you want to start completely from scratch on your iPhone and reset it back to its factory defaults, tap on the Settings app, then tap General. You will see a **Reset button** at the bottom of the General screen. Tap Reset and you can choose to Reset All Settings, Erase All Content and Settings, Reset Network Settings, Reset Keyboard Dictionary, Reset Home Screen Layout, or Reset Location & Privacy. The two main ones that you'll want to choose from are Reset All Settings and Erase All Content and Settings. The first choice (Reset All Settings) will reset all your settings and preferences but leave your data and media intact, so you will still have all your contacts, calendars, songs, etc. The second option (Erase All Content and Settings) is the one that will reset your iPhone back to its factory defaults and wipe out everything you put on it.

Can't Make Calls

If you want to make a call, your iPhone has to be active and there has to be a cellular network in range. Your carrier's name should be displayed in the upper-left corner, along with your current signal strength. If you're roaming on another provider's network, you should see that network's name. If you don't see a network name or you see No Service, then you will not be able to make calls until you are back in the range of a wireless carrier. Also, if you have traveled outside of your country's home network, you may not be set up for international roaming. Check with your carrier to make sure that your account has international roaming. Also, make sure you're not in Airplane mode. If there is a little icon of a plane in the upper-left corner of the screen, then you are in Airplane mode and will not be able to make calls until you turn it off in the Settings app.

---

iTip **Your iPhone Can Cause Interference**

*If you have other wireless devices in your home/office, such as cordless phones, speaker systems, video/audio recording equipment, etc., the iPhone's transceiver could cause audible interference (buzzing) on them. You can usually cure it by going to Settings and turning on **Airplane Mode**. However, note that while your iPhone is in Airplane mode, you will not be able to make or receive calls or texts, or access the Internet.*

Did Your App Crash?

Not all apps are created equally, so you may have an app crash now and then. The good thing is that the iPhone operating system (iOS) is based upon Mac OS X, which is really reliable. So even if an app crashes, it usually won't affect the rest of the iPhone and will simply return you to the Home screen. However, if the app just appears frozen and not responding, then you can manually force quit it by pressing-and-holding the **Sleep/Wake button** at the top of the iPhone until the red button with "Slide to Power Off" appears. Then press-and-hold the **Home button** on the front of the iPhone for at least six seconds, and you should be returned to the Home screen.

Poorly Running Apps

If you have an app that isn't frozen, but appears to be running poorly, or you just want to start it up from a cold start, then you'll need to manually quit it. Double-click the Home button to bring up the multitasking bar. Scroll along the bar (by swiping side-ways) until you see the app that you want to quit, and then press-and-hold on it like you're rearranging your apps on your Home screen. All of the apps in the multitasking bar will start to wiggle, and a – **(minus sign) button** will appear in the upper-left corner of each one. Just tap that button on the app you want to quit. Now you can press the Home button again and relaunch the app, if you like.

Do a Backup and Restore

If your iPhone is misbehaving or just plain acting weird, it may be time to do a restore. You'll need to sync your iPhone before doing this so that it is backed up. Once the sync is done, leave your iPhone connected to your computer and click the **Restore button** on the Summary pane in your iPhone's preferences in iTunes. This will reinstall the current iPhone firmware on your iPhone and then do a restore of your data from the backup. This can easily take 20 minutes or more, so make sure you do it when you have time to be without your iPhone.

Battery Saving Tips

Your iPhone's battery life is going to depend on how you use it. Any one of these tips will help, but the more of them you use, the longer your battery will go between charges.

Keep your iPhone out of the sun. This is one of the most important things you can do to conserve battery life. Heat will affect your battery the most, so try not to leave it in any hot places, like your car's glove box.

Try reducing the screen brightness. The screen is one of the main sources for drawing power. If you reduce the brightness, the iPhone will use less battery power. You can do this from the Settings screen.

Turn off Wi-Fi and Bluetooth, if not needed. If you're in an area that doesn't have Wi-Fi, or you're traveling in and out of hotspots, then there is no reason to have your iPhone constantly searching for a network to connect to. Turn off Wi-Fi from the Settings screen. If you're not using your Bluetooth headset, you can turn that off, too (also from the Settings screen). With these radios off, the iPhone will also charge faster.

Let your battery run completely down. As with most electronic devices that use rechargeable batteries, it's always a good idea to let your battery run completely down occasionally before recharging. Think of it as exorcising the battery and prolonging its life, as well.

More Battery Saving Tips

Here are a couple more options to save battery life: If you're not actively in a 3G or 4G LTE (only on iPhone 5) coverage area, having 3G/4G LTE on will drain your battery faster as your iPhone continues to look for 3G/4G LTE coverage. Turn off **Enable 3G** on an iPhone 4 (this is not available on an iPhone 4S) or **Enable LTE** on an iPhone 5 in the Cellular settings in the General settings of the Settings app. Also, if you're having your data (such as email, and calendar and contact updates) "pushed," then you can switch from Push to Fetch. This will bring in your data on a timed interval, as opposed to every second of the day. I found that turning off Push gave me a drastic improvement on my iPhone's battery life. You can turn Push off by tapping Settings and then tapping Mail, Contacts, Calendars, then **Fetch New Data**. Lastly, if you don't need the location services (geotagging your photos, GPS, etc.), you can also extend your battery life by turning **Location Services** off in the Privacy settings of the Settings app.

SIM Card Not Detected by Your iPhone

SIM tray

iPhone 4/4S   iPhone 5

The iPhone is a GSM-based phone, so it comes with a SIM card already installed in it. If your iPhone isn't seeing the SIM card, try removing it and re-seating it. Using a small paper clip, insert one end in the hole on the SIM tray and press firmly until the tray pops up. Make sure there is no dirt or debris on it and try putting it back in. The SIM tray on the iPhone 5, 4S, and 4 is located on the side. *Note:* The iPhone 4 and 4S use a micro-SIM card, so it's not compatible with regular SIM slots unless you have an adapter tray. You can get an adapter tray on Amazon.com, if you ever need to put your SIM card in another phone. The iPhone 5 uses a nano-SIM card and it's also not compatible with other iPhone models without an adapter tray.

---

iTip **Remove Your SIM Card When Servicing**

If you ever have to send your iPhone in for service, you can remove the SIM card and try it in another GSM-based phone (this way, you'll still have use of a cell phone while yours is being serviced. But, as I mentioned above, you'll need an adapter tray). Apple doesn't require your SIM card to service your phone and, as a matter of fact, they request that you remove it before you send it in anyway.

Software Updates Are Important

Every now and then, problems will be addressed in software updates for both your iPhone and your apps. If you're experiencing problems, make sure you're on the latest version of your iOS, and that you've updated your apps to their latest versions. To check for iOS updates, tap on the Settings app, then tap on General, and tap on **Software Update**. To check for app updates, tap on App Store on the Home screen, and then tap on **Updates** at the bottom right.

Problems Downloading or Updating Apps, Music, etc.

If, all of a sudden, you are having problems downloading or updating apps, music, or other iTunes content on your iPhone, try signing out and then back into your iTunes & App Stores account. Tap iTunes & App Stores in the Settings app and then tap on your Apple ID (email address) at the top of the screen. When the menu pops up, tap **Sign Out**. Then, enter your Apple ID and password again to log back in. Once you're logged back in, try your download again.

Chapter Sixteen

Matchbox Twenty

20 Apps We Can't Live Without

Okay, so you might be thinking, "Really? The band Matchbox Twenty? That is soooooo year 2000." And you would be right, if they hadn't just reunited for a new album with a breakout hit song on it called "She's So Mean," which is the story of a girl who won't let her boyfriend download any cool apps and forces him to instead use just the apps that came pre-installed on his iPhone 5. Now, when you first read that you might be thinking, "Man, that's cruel!" But, then that makes you want to jump over to the iTunes app to buy Bobby Brown's hit "Don't Be Cruel," from back in 1988, where it spent a whopping 11 non-consecutive weeks at the top of the Billboard charts, which I know is something you were secretly hoping to learn today. Anyway, let's circle back to the mean girl and her limited-app hang-up. Here's the thing: A lot of folks have lost all recollection that when the original iPhone shipped, just a few years back, there was no such thing as "downloadable" apps. That's right, you had the apps that came pre-installed on your iPhone and that was it. There was no App Store back then (that came later). So, it was just Stocks, Weather, Mail, and so on, and people were literally thrilled to have them, which is probably why I heard that Matchbox Twenty is considering re-releasing "She's So Mean" as "She's Not as Bad as I Thought" (although *Rolling Stone* magazine leaked that they were also considering "She's a Little Bit Pesky," but when they heard the rumor that Bobby Brown was then considering re-releasing "Don't Be Cruel" as "Don't Be a Little Bit Pesky," they changed their minds). Anyway, now downloadable apps are a part of our lives. So much so that Terry and I thought we'd share 20 of the apps that we just can't live without, even though we obviously managed to live without downloadable apps for a while there, but now we're spoiled (although I prefer the term "pesky").

Yahoo! Sportacular

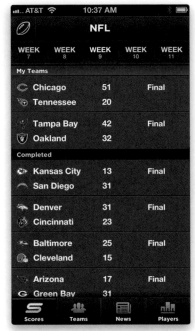

There are a lot of apps out there that give you the latest sports scores and, of course, Yahoo! Sportacular does a great job of that (it really has a fantastic interface and all-around user experience). But, the app is so much more than that, because if you can't watch the game on TV or on the web, this is the next best thing. It has game previews, loads of stats on…well…everything for about every sport you can think of, and it has got lots of team and player news, as well. But, best of all, it has play-by-play coverage for many sporting events, so you can follow right along as the plays happen and you can set it up to get in-game alerts (so if your team scores, it can alert you even if you're not using the app at that moment). Plus, it's just plain fast, which I love! Want to love it even more? It's free. —Scott

Zite Personalized Magazine

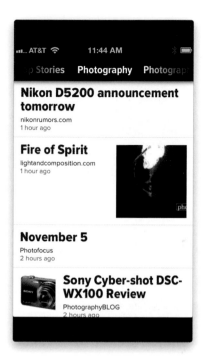

Zite Personalized Magazine is a news aggregator that is so handy and popular that CNN actually bought it. You choose the topics that interest you, and it brings you lots of news, with photos, on those topics. I look at it daily for photography news and it always seems to uncover news I would have otherwise missed. It has a simple, elegant interface that makes getting news on your interests fun and fast, plus it's free (which is a really great price).—Scott

Reeder

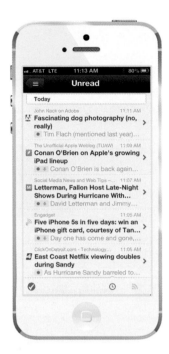

I don't get the local newspaper delivered to me, and I don't go to any one site for news each day. However, I have a lot of sites that I follow via their RSS feeds. Google Reader is my choice for keeping these feeds organized and the Reeder app ($2.99 in the App Store) is my go-to app throughout the day. It syncs with Google Reader, so I can check my news feeds on any of my devices at any time. Once I mark stories I've read as read, they are marked read on all of my devices.—Terry

Flipboard: Your Social News Magazine

Two years ago, Flipboard: Your Social News Magazine was Apple's own pick for "iPad App of the Year" and rightly so. But, at the time, it was only available for the iPad. Now, there's a free iPhone version and it's one of those apps I use multiple times every single day. It takes your social media accounts (like Facebook, Twitter, etc.) and displays them as if they were a magazine, showing the photos and images associated with a link big and beautiful, and it makes all your social media look infinitely more interesting (you'll find it hard to go back to seeing just the text version of Twitter, or the tiny images on Facebook). It's really just beautifully designed and I think it's one of the best apps ever! You can also add other popular news feeds or blogs and have them displayed graphically in Flipboard, as well, but I think it's your social media feeds that'll make you fall in love.—Scott

Tweetbot for Twitter

The native Twitter client keeps getting better, but I still prefer the interface of the Tweetbot for Twitter app on my iPhone ($2.99 in the App Store). Tweetbot supports bit.ly links, whereas Twitter does not. Twitter wants to lock you in to their services, such as the picture service and URL shortener; Tweetbot allows you to choose the services that you want to use with Twitter, so that you can do your own tracking and management, instead of handing that all over to Twitter. I also like the fact that it syncs with iCloud across your devices and even Tweetbot for Mac. That way, you don't waste any time reading or responding to tweets that you already read or responded to.—Terry

Foursquare

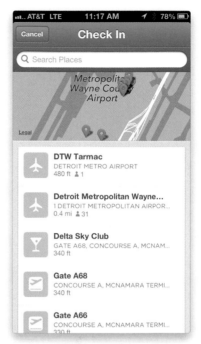

While I do enjoy social media networks to interact with friends and fans, I restrict check-ins on Foursquare to people I actually know (like close friends and family). The free Foursquare app is fun—it's fun competing for those meaningless points just to be ahead of your other Foursquare friends. I also like checking in to unusual places. And, you can post photos of your check-ins and simultaneously post your status updates to Twitter or Facebook.—Terry

Instagram

I'm late to the Instagram party, because I really didn't see a reason to be on yet another social network. However, what I like most about the free Instagram app is that I can post images simultaneously to Instagram, Facebook, Twitter, Flickr, email them, and check in to Foursquare. Think of Instagram as "visual status updates." You can also enhance your pictures with filters and your news feed will show you pictures posted by the people you follow in a nice easy-to-view manner. You can "Like" them and/or comment on them, too.—Terry

Adobe Revel

The built-in Photos app is great, and so is the ability to use Photo Stream. This is all fine and good if you use Apple's iPhoto or Aperture on your Mac or the Pictures Library on your PC. My photo libraries, though, all exist primarily within Adobe Lightroom, and with the built-in Adobe Revel support, I can sync my photos to the cloud and then automatically to all my Macs and iOS devices. Revel has become the way that I easily take my photography with me, so that I can show it off even if I'm offline. Also, unlike Photo Stream, there is no limit to the number of photos that you can have in your Adobe Revel account. While the Adobe Revel app is free, Adobe Revel is a paid service ($5.99/month) with unlimited storage.—Terry

Uber

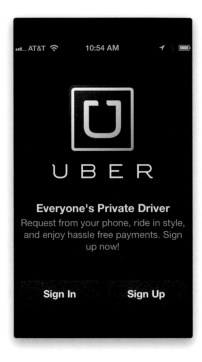

This may be my new favorite app (you'll have to read to the end to find out why). First, you create an account and enter your credit card and phone number (I know, that sounds bad, but it's awesome!). Then, the next time you need a ride and don't want to cram into the back of a hot, dirty taxi, you launch the Uber app. It finds your location and it tells you how many minutes away the closest black Lincoln Town Car or black SUV is from your location (in my experience, one's about 4–6 minutes away in most cities). You tap Set Pickup Location and, in literally seconds, you get a message with the driver's name, description of the car, the driver's star rating, license plate number, and how long until he arrives. Then, it shows a black car on a map heading your way, so you can track its progress. When it arrives, you get a text saying it's there, the driver opens your door, gets your bag, etc., and there's a bottle of water waiting for you inside. The cars are very clean, and the drivers are extremely friendly, because you get to give them a star rating right in the app, along with comments if you like. When you arrive at your destination, they open your door, you just say "Thanks," and you're on your way. You don't hand him any money, you don't figure out the tip, it's automatically billed to your Uber account, and you get a detailed receipt emailed within just a few minutes, giving you every possible statistic (including a map of your route and a photo of the driver). Best of all, it's just a little more than a regular taxi (I called an Uber car recently, but there were too many of us to fit, so half our group went in a taxi instead. The taxi was $15. Our Uber car was $18, and we didn't have a story about the smell or how the taxi driver wouldn't turn on the air conditioning and then said he couldn't take a credit card). It's not in every city yet, but it's in a bunch (I even used it in Paris recently), and it's free.—Scott

TripIt – Travel Organizer

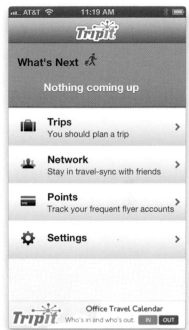

If you're tired of digging through your emails to find the one with your flight times or gate number, and if you have to pull out your laptop to find your hotel confirmation number when you check in, you are going to so love TripIt! When a travel-related email comes in, you just forward it to "plans@tripit.com" and it reads the document and puts it right into your app in a very easy-to-read, clean, large format that makes finding things like your boarding gate, flight time, hotel location, and more so incredibly easy. Once you've used TripIt, you can't imagine living without it. Very well designed, free (or $3.99 for the version with no ads), and a zillion fans make this one of my "must-have" apps for travelers.—Scott

FlightTrack Pro – Live Flight Status Tracker

My job requires that I fly quite a bit and, while I can have apps for each airline on my iPhone, FlightTrack Pro ($9.99 in the App Store) is my one-stop shop for any of my flights on any airline. While I don't fly every single day, I do fly often enough to depend on Flight-Track Pro to keep me updated on any last minute flight/gate changes via push notifications. It has saved me on more than one occasion. Best of all, it syncs with TripIt, so my flights are automatically loaded into the app via the cloud.—Terry

GateGuru, Airport Info & Flight Status

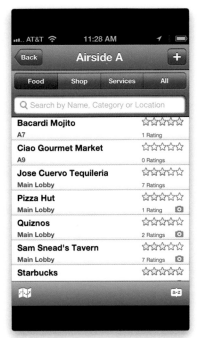

This is another free one for travelers, and it's another one you'll wonder how you lived without, especially if you do a lot of air travel. It's called GateGuru and, when you launch it, it finds out which airport you're in and shows you, concourse by concourse, a list of all the restaurants, shops, and services (including airline club lounges), with a map of where they all are, plus ratings and reviews. That way, you don't wind up eating at McDonalds, because you didn't know that three gates down was a Nature's Table Bistro (try the one in Atlanta's Concourse E—they have really great fresh sandwiches, hot dishes, and wonderful salads). The app is also great for finding airport ATMs, restrooms, you name it.—Scott

NAVIGON

While it's great having a built-in GPS in my car at home, I don't usually have that advantage when I travel. So, rather than having to pay a daily rental fee or having to travel with another device, I use my iPhone for GPS turn-by-turn directions. I've tried several of these kinds of apps and even the new Maps app in iOS 6, but I find NAVIGON (the NAVIGON North America app is $59.99 in the App Store) to be the best. It's constantly updated with new features, and the maps exist on your iPhone, so that you can continue navigating even if you're not online. In the latest version for North America, you can download just the apps for the states you need to save space on your iPhone. NAVIGON also has integrated Google Local Search for quickly finding and navigating to local points of interest. It has all the features I could imagine, and even rivals the one built-in to my car at home. When I travel, I don't think twice about using the NAVIGON app in my rental car.—Terry

TomTom

iOS 6 does come with built-in turn-by-turn navigation in the Maps app, but once you've used TomTom (an iPhone version of the popular hardware navigation system), you get really spoiled. I used to rent a nav system when I rented a car (at about $9–$12 a day), but since I got TomTom, I've saved a ton of money and untold frustration. I also have the excellent NAVIGON navigation app, but I always wind up coming back to TomTom, because it's so easy to use, easy to see, and it does a great job overall. Although these nav systems' days may be numbered as Apple improves the turn-by-turn navigation in the Maps app, for now, TomTom is still king of the hill and highly recommended. The price varies depending on the region you need (the TomTom U.S.A. app is $49.99).—Scott

Movies by Flixster

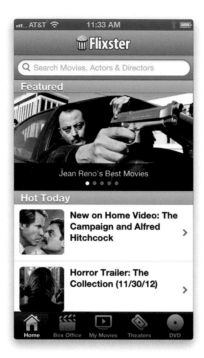

I've tried just about every movie time app out there, and I still haven't found anything that touches Movies by Flixster. You can choose which local theaters you want as favorites, so their show times show up first, and can you do everything from watch movie trailers (right in the app), to read Rotten Tomatoes reviews, and even buy tickets. Very complete and well designed, and it's free!—Scott

Presentation Clock

This app, from my buddy and ace app designer Shawn Welch, is a slick countdown clock for anyone who has to do presentations or talks of any kind. You simply choose the length of time your presentation is supposed to last and then you choose two warning times. For example, I like to know when there are 15 minutes left in my session, so when that point occurs, Presentation Clock makes an audible warning sound, and the numbers on my large countdown clock turn yellow (perfect color for a warning, right?). Then, I like another warning when there are just 5 minutes left, so when I get down to there, I get another audible warning sound and the numbers turn red (a more serious warning). Then, if I run over, the screen inverts to let me know I've gone over my time, but it keeps counting to let me know how much I'm over. You can save presets for different length presentations, so just one tap and you're ready to go. He makes an iPad version, too, in case you really, really need glasses (LOL!). This one's just 99¢.—Scott

1Password

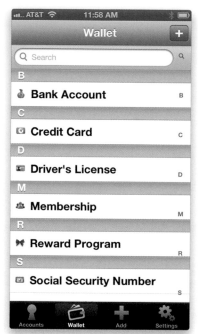

Managing all your passwords, across multiple websites, and credit cards, and accounts can be a nightmare. Well, at least without 1Password it can be. This is the ultimate password app and you can sync it between not only your mobile devices, but your desktop app, as well. So, if you add a new password on one device, it appears in 1Password on all your devices. Plus, it's brilliant at generating secure unique passwords for you on the fly. Great interface and easy to use; you'll wonder how your brain held all this stuff without it. It's only $9.99 for the iPhone and iPod touch or $14.99 for the iPhone, iPod touch, and iPad.—Scott

Starbucks

Believe it or not, I never had a cup of coffee before two years ago—always loved the smell, but hated the taste. I have grown to like lattes, and since Starbucks is just about every-where I go, I can get a consistent experience/taste. The free Starbucks app lets me fuel my Starbucks card, find locations, and now with Passbook support, I like it even more. When I'm near any of my favorite Starbucks locations, my Starbucks pass automatically pops up on my Lock screen. I just swipe to unlock and there is my Starbucks pass in Passbook ready to scan at the register.—Terry

Dropbox

 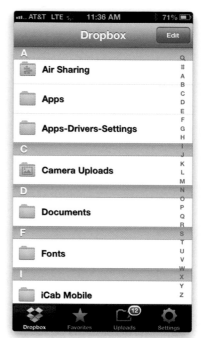

Dropbox is crucial in my day-to-day workflow, so having the Dropbox app on my iPhone means that I always have access to all of my documents, other files, photos, etc. I now use the Camera Upload feature to automatically upload photos and screenshots that I take with my iOS devices to Dropbox and, therefore, my computer. You can go to the Dropbox website and sign up for a free account with at least 2 GB of free space. Then, download the free Dropbox app and you're all set to access the same files on both your computer and your iPhone.—Terry

Delivery Status Touch, a Package Tracker

It seems like I'm always either shipping something to someone or waiting for a shipment from someone. There is no better app than Delivery Status to track all your deliveries from various providers, such as FedEx, UPS, USPS, DHL, etc. Delivery Status ($4.99 in the App Store) can show you a summary of all your packages at once. You can see where they were last scanned and when they are expected to be delivered. At any time, you can tap to actually go to the carrier's tracking website right within the app. This is great when you want details, like who signed for the package or what the problem is if it wasn't delivered. —Terry

Note: Be sure to check out Terry's Best App Site website (www.bestappsite.com) regularly. There, he reviews the best apps found in the App Store.

Index

Reply with Message button, 41, 311
Reset screen, 278, 332
resetting your iPhone, 332
restoring data from backups, 180, 336
Restrictions settings, 295
returning missed calls, 35
Revel, Adobe, 351
Ring/Silent switch, 5, 44, 234, 271, 327
Ringer volume slider, 44, 306
ringtones
   assigning to callers, 46
   choosing for your iPhone, 45, 306
   creating your own, 275–276
roaming, 274, 298, 333
Rule of Thirds grid, 226

S

Safari web browser, 113–130
   bookmarks, 99, 119–121
   browsing history in, 264
   dialing numbers from, 127
   email links opening, 99
   entering addresses into, 114, 117, 120
   filling in forms using, 128
   full-screen browsing mode in, 263
   getting a new webpage in, 117
   Google search engine and, 124
   iCloud tabs and, 123
   launching, 114
   navigating webpages in, 115, 118
   opening links in, 116, 127
   printing webpages from, 130
   Private Browsing option, 129
   Reader button, 126
   Reading List, 116
   refreshing webpages in, 119
   saving/copying images with, 129
   setting options for, 315
   sharing webpages with, 130
   uploading photos with, 265
   web clips and, 122
   See also webpages
Satellite view, 149, 152
Save to Camera Roll button, 96, 251
scheduling appointments, 161
Scientific Calculator, 144

screen options
   brightness settings, 307, 337
   screen orientation lock, 208
   stopping auto-rotation, 240
screenshots, 281
scrolling, 3
scrubbing feature, 200
search engine setting, 124, 315
searching
   contacts, 19
   email messages, 103
   Maps, 145, 148
   music/songs, 192
   settings for, 301
   text messages, 64
   the web, 124
self-portraits, 226
settings, 289–321
   Accessibility, 305
   Airplane mode, 290
   calendar, 309
   Cellular, 298
   contact, 309
   Do Not Disturb, 293
   email, 309
   Facebook, 321
   FaceTime, 48, 313
   general, 295
   iCloud, 180
   International, 304
   iTunes & App Stores, 316
   Keyboard, 295, 303
   Location Services, 308
   Maps app, 314
   Messages app, 312
   Music app, 317
   Notes app, 310
   Notifications, 294
   Personal Hotspot, 299
   Phone app, 311
   Photos & Camera, 319
   Privacy, 308
   Safari browser, 315
   screen brightness, 307
   Sounds, 44, 306
   Spotlight search, 301
   text message, 312